TO DAVE
FROM DAD

Other books by David L. Nichols:

Understanding the Old Testament: A Narrative Summary
(CreateSpace Publishing, 2008)

Learning to Love Your Neighbor: Finding Your Place in God's Plan to Fix a Broken World
(CreateSpace Publishing, 2014)

All titles available through: www.amazon.com

Encountering Jesus Today:

Revolution and Resurrection

David L. Nichols

Encountering Jesus Today: Revolution and Resurrection

Unless indicated otherwise, all scripture passages are quotations from or paraphrases of:

World English Bible (WEB), public domain

ISBN-10: 1537705636

ISBN-13: 978-1537705637

Printed in the U.S.A.

CreateSpace

4900 LaCross Road

North Charleston, SC 29406

For additional information:

EncounteringJesusToday@gmail.com

Contents

Why Jesus?

There are 2.2 billion Christians today who worship Jesus as the world's Savior and another 1.6 billion Muslims who honor him as a prophet of God. It is hard to imagine who else could be called "the most honored man who ever lived."

This, of course, doesn't prove anything, but it does suggest spending a little time learning about Jesus could be good.

Although Jesus lived 2,000 years ago, his world was not so different from our own. Of course, they didn't have the "benefits" of technology we have, but their problems weren't much different: greed and corruption; hatred and violence; oppression and injustice; prejudice and bigotry; fear and distrust, and on and on.

During Jesus' life, the Roman Empire was at its peak. Rome was the largest city in the world and the empire was the world's only superpower. The Pax Romana (Roman peace) had begun a generation before the birth of Jesus and would continue after his death for two centuries throughout the western world. The one exception to this Roman stability was the Mideast, which was a powder keg of religious and political unrest. Jewish-Roman wars erupted about thirty years after Jesus died, and continued on and off for sixty years until every remnant of the Jewish temple had been obliterated, Jerusalem was in ruins, and the majority of the Jews who survived were dispersed throughout the world.

For decades before the wars began, the Jewish people had seethed with frustration and despair under Roman rule. They had difficulty thinking of themselves as God's Chosen People when God was allowing them to be ruled by emperors who outrageously proclaimed themselves divine, taxed everyone endlessly and sold the office of chief priest each year to the highest bidder.

With the exception of those who benefited from Roman rule, the Jews longed for the days when prophets like Elijah proclaimed God's judgment on evildoers, priests like Aaron interceded for them with God, and kings like David ruled with righteousness and justice.

This was the world to which Jesus came as a new kind of prophet, priest and king, who declared himself to be the fulfillment of ancient prophecies. He raised the hopes of those who longed for a better world, and incurred the wrath of those who had power and privilege in the world as it was.

Revolution and the Kingdom of God

The revolution Jesus proclaimed was not what anyone expected. He lived a simple and humble life, but was accused of partying too much and spending too much time with the most outrageous social outcasts. He was wildly popular because of the people he healed and the miracles he performed, but he made lots of enemies by refusing to abide by accepted rules and customs.

His revolution was totally out of step with the world because he advocated outrageous love (even for enemies!) and humble service. He said a day was coming in which the rich and powerful would be judged for all their misdeeds, and those who were victims of oppression and abuse would finally see justice done.

Not surprisingly, the powers that be decided Jesus could not be allowed to continue promoting such a revolution. They determined he must be silenced. Permanently. The chosen form of punishment, crucifixion, was notorious for its cruelty.

The death of Jesus should have been the end of the story. It wasn't.

Resurrection and the Kingdom of God

The resurrection Jesus experienced was even more unexpected than the revolutionary kingdom he proclaimed. It demonstrated nothing less than the power of God to defeat the forces of evil and death itself.

The resurrection of Jesus re-energized his band of followers who had given up all hope. Within a matter of days they went from being afraid to even be seen in public, to the place where they boldly proclaimed the resurrection and ended up sacrificing their lives rather than being willing to recant their testimony.

An invitation

In many ways, the story of Jesus began long before the gospels were written and continued long after his crucifixion and resurrection. The scope of this book, though, is the period covered by the Bible's four gospels: Matthew, Mark, Luke and John. It begins with stories of his birth and ends with appearances to his disciples in the days following the resurrection.

This book blends the Bible's four gospels into one story. Each section contains a text box with information to help you encounter Jesus through what you read. The footnotes reference the books, chapters and verses on which each section is based.

I welcome your comments and questions, and will respond as time and energy allow. Feel free to contact me by email:

EncounteringJesusToday@gmail.com

David L. Nichols
November 2016

Chapter 1: Beginnings

Introduction[1]

The beginning of the good news of Jesus Christ, the Son of God. Many have undertaken to write an account of what has happened among us, even as those who from the beginning were eye-witnesses told us. It seemed good to me also, most honorable Theophilus, having traced the course of all things from the start, to write this that you might know with certainty what you were taught.

Theophilus may or may not be an actual person's name; in Greek it simply means "lover of God." Do you think of yourself as a lover of God? Where have you learned about Jesus?

Prayer: Open my heart and mind, Lord, to discover the good news of Jesus in all its history-changing wonder.

Overview[2]

In the beginning was the Word, and the Word was with God, and the Word was God. He was in the beginning with God; all things were made through him. In him was life, and the life was the light of all. The light shines in the darkness; the darkness hasn't overcome it.

There was a man named John who was sent from God. He came as a witness, to testify about the light, that all might believe through him. He was not the light, but the true light that enlightens everyone was coming into the world.

The true light was in the world which had been made through him, and yet it didn't recognize him. Even those who were his own didn't receive him when he came to them, but he gave to as many as did receive him, who believed in his name, the right to become God's children, born not of human desire, but born of God.

---

1 Mark 1:1; Luke 1:1-4
2 John 1:1-18

The Word became flesh, and lived among us. We saw his glory as the only Son of the Father, full of grace and truth. John testified about him, saying, "This was the one of whom I said, 'He who comes after me is above me because he was before me.'" From his fullness we've all received grace upon grace. The law was given through Moses; grace and truth came through Jesus Christ. No one has seen God at any time. The one and only Son, who is in the heart of the Father, has made him known.

According to Genesis 1, creation began with God speaking these words: "Let there be light." By picking up themes of creation, word, and light, the gospel writer confronts the reader with the idea this is not just another story about just another man: it is the story of life itself. How do you react to that?

Prayer: Clean out the clutter of my life, Lord, to make space for grace and truth.

The Birth of John Foretold[3]

In the time of King Herod of Judea there was a priest named Zechariah, whose wife, Elizabeth, was also a descendant of Aaron. Both of them were righteous in God's sight, obeying the Lord's commands and decrees blamelessly. They were very old, and childless because Elizabeth was unable to conceive.

Once when Zechariah's division was on duty, he was chosen to go into the temple of the Lord and burn incense. When the time came, all the assembled worshipers were praying outside.

An angel of the Lord appeared to him, standing at the right side of the altar. When Zechariah saw him, he was startled and gripped with fear. But the angel said: "Do not be afraid, Zechariah; your prayer has been heard. Your wife Elizabeth will bear you a son, and you are to call him John. He will be a joy and delight to you, and many will rejoice because of his birth, for he will be great in the sight of the Lord. He is never to take wine or other fermented drink, and he will be filled with the Holy Spirit even before he is born. He will bring back many of the people of Israel to the Lord their God. And he will go on before the Lord, in the spirit and power of Elijah, to turn the hearts of parents to their children and the disobedient to the wisdom of the righteous, preparing people for the coming of the Lord."

---

[3] Luke 1:5-25

Zechariah asked the angel, "How can I believe this? I am an old man and my wife is well along in years."

The angel said to him, "I am Gabriel. I stand in the presence of God, and have been sent to tell you this good news. Now you will be silent, unable to speak until the day this happens, because you did not believe my words, which will come true at their appointed time."

Meanwhile, the people were waiting for Zechariah and wondering why he stayed so long in the temple. When he came out, he could not speak to them. They realized he had seen a vision in the temple, for he kept making signs to them but was unable to speak.

When his time of service was completed, Zechariah returned home. After this, Elizabeth became pregnant and for five months remained in seclusion. "The Lord has done this for me," she said. "In these days he has shown his favor and taken away my disgrace among the people."

As a priest, Zechariah would have known of many miracles God had performed throughout history. It was another matter, though to believe God could do a miracle in his own life. Do you have difficulty imagining God at work in your life? When you reflect back over the past, can you see God's hand in what seemed at the time random acts or even tragic situations?

Prayer: Help me remember, Lord: if you are real, miracles can happen.

The Birth of Jesus Foretold[4]

In the sixth month, the angel Gabriel was sent from God to Nazareth, a city of Galilee, to Mary, who was pledged to be married to Joseph, a descendant of David. The angel said to her, "Rejoice, highly favored one! The Lord is with you. Blessed are you among women!"

When she saw the angel, Mary was greatly troubled, and wondered what kind of greeting this might be. The angel said to her, "Don't be afraid, Mary, for you have found favor with God. You will conceive, and give birth to a son, and will call his name 'Jesus.' He will be great, and will be called the Son of the Most High. The Lord God will give him the throne of

---

Both Mary and Zechariah had questions when told by Gabriel of an impending miraculous birth. There was a difference, though, between their responses: Mary didn't understand; Zechariah didn't believe. If you had a message from God, would you respond more like Mary or Zechariah?

Prayer: Help my faithfulness, Lord, not be limited by my need to understand.

---

[4] Luke 1:26-38

his father, David, and he will reign over the house of Jacob forever; there will be no end to his kingdom."

Mary said to the angel, "How can this be, since I am a virgin?"

The angel answered, "The Holy Spirit will come on you, and the power of the Most High will overshadow you. The holy one born in you will be called the Son of God. Elizabeth, your relative, also has conceived a son in her old age; this is the sixth month with her who was called barren. Nothing said by God is impossible."

Mary said, "I am the servant of the Lord; let it be done to me as you have said."

Mary's Visit to Elizabeth[5]

The angel departed and Mary arose and went into the hill country to the house of Zechariah. When Elizabeth heard Mary's greeting, the baby leaped in her womb, and Elizabeth was filled with the Holy Spirit. She called out with a loud voice, "Blessed are you among women, and blessed is the fruit of your womb! Why am I so favored, that the mother of my Lord should come to me? When the voice of your greeting came to my ears, the baby leaped in my womb for joy! Blessed is she who believed, for there will be a fulfillment of the things spoken to her from the Lord!"

Mary said,

"My soul magnifies the Lord.
My spirit has rejoiced in God my Savior,
for he has looked at the humble state of his servant.
From now on, all generations will call me blessed.
For he who is mighty has done great things for me.
Holy is his name.
His mercy is for generations of generations to those who fear him.
He has shown strength with his arm.
He has scattered the proud in the imagination of their hearts.

The Bible doesn't say why Mary visited Elizabeth, but part of the reason had to be their shared experience of miraculous pregnancies. How often must they have said to each other, "Can you believe this is really happening?" Have you ever had a profound sense of wonder at God's presence in your life? Did you tell someone about it?

Prayer: Remind me, Lord, that my intimate moments with you are to be shared with others, not kept to myself.

[5] Luke 1:39-56

He has put down princes from their thrones.
He has exalted the lowly.
He has filled the hungry with good things.
He has sent the rich away empty.
He has given help to Israel, his servant, that he might remember mercy,
as he spoke to our fathers,
to Abraham and his offspring forever."

Mary stayed with her about three months, and then returned to her house.

The Birth of John[6]

When the time came for Elizabeth to give birth, her neighbors and her relatives rejoiced with her at the Lord's mercy. On the eighth day, they came to circumcise the child; they would have called him Zechariah, after his father, but his mother said, "No; he will be called John."

They said to her, "There is no one among your relatives who is called by this name." They made signs to his father, to learn what he would have him called.

He asked for a writing tablet, and wrote, "His name is John."

They all marveled. His tongue was freed immediately, and he spoke, blessing God. Amazement came on all who lived around them, and all these sayings were talked about throughout the hill country of Judea. All who heard remembered, saying, because the hand of the Lord was with him, "What will this child be?" Zechariah, filled with the Holy Spirit, prophesied, "Blessed be the Lord, the God of Israel, for he has visited us to redeem his people. He has raised up a horn of salvation for us in the house of his servant David as foretold by ancient prophets. He has given us salvation from our enemies, and from the hand of all who hate us. He has shown mercy to our fathers, remembering his holy covenant. He has fulfilled the oath he spoke to Abraham that we, being delivered out of the hand of our

---

In the course of nine months or so, Zechariah went from doubt to ecstasy. Maybe some of his enthusiasm at the birth of his son came from having been silent for so long. Have you ever known anyone with aphasia, the inability to speak, perhaps due to a stroke or other cause? Do you value your ability to speak, choosing your words wisely?

Prayer: May the words of my mouth, Lord, consistently express the joy of my life rather than its irritation.

---

[6] Luke 1:57-80

enemies, should serve him without fear, in holiness and righteousness all the days of our lives. And you, child, will be called a prophet of the Most High, for you will go before the Lord to prepare his ways, to give knowledge of salvation to his people by the forgiveness of their sins, because of the tender mercy of our God, whereby the dawn from on high will visit us, to shine on those who sit in darkness and the shadow of death, to guide our feet into the way of peace."

The child grew, becoming strong in spirit, and was in the desert until the day of his public appearance to Israel.

The Birth of Jesus[7]

The birth of Jesus, happened like this: after his mother, Mary, was engaged to Joseph, she became pregnant. Joseph, being a righteous man, and not wanting to make a public example of Mary, considered ending the relationship quietly. As he thought about this, an angel of the Lord appeared to him in a dream, saying, "Joseph, son of David, don't be afraid to take Mary to be your wife, for what is conceived in her is of the Holy Spirit. She shall give birth to a son. You shall call him Jesus, for he will save his people from their sins."

Joseph faced a huge dilemma when he learned of Mary's pregnancy. He must have felt torn between the unthinkable and the unbelievable. The message from the angel didn't promise an easy path, but at least the right thing to do became clear. What have been some of the most difficult decisions you've had to make? Have you sensed God making it clear to you what was the right thing to do even when it wasn't easy?

Prayer: When I'm faced with impossible choices, Lord, show me the way to go.

This happened, to fulfill what was said by the Lord through a prophet:

"Behold, the virgin shall be with child,
and shall give birth to a son.
They shall call his name Immanuel,
which means, "God with us."

Joseph arose from his sleep, ready to do as the angel of the Lord commanded: he would take Mary to be his wife, and would not sleep with her until she had given birth to her firstborn son.

Some months later, a decree went out from Caesar Augustus that the world should be taxed, and all went to their ancestral city to be enrolled. Joseph went from Nazareth in Galilee, to Bethlehem in Judea, the city of David, his ancestor, to be enrolled with Mary.

[7] Matthew 1:18-25; Luke 2:1-7

While they were there, the day came for her to give birth to her firstborn son. She wrapped him in bands of cloth, and laid him in a manger, because there was no room for them in the inn.

The Shepherds' Surprise[8]

There were shepherds out in the fields near Bethlehem, keeping watch at night over their flock. Suddenly, an angel of the Lord stood by them, and the glory of the Lord shone around them, and they were terrified. The angel said to them, "Don't be afraid. I bring you good news of great joy which will be to all the people. There is born to you today, in David's city, a Savior, who is Christ, the Lord. This is the sign to you: you will find a baby wrapped in strips of cloth, lying in a manger." Suddenly, there was with the angel a multitude of the heavenly host praising God, and saying,

"Glory to God in the highest,
on earth peace, good will toward all."

When the angels left, the shepherds said, "Let's go to Bethlehem, and see this thing that has happened, which the Lord has made known to us." They went quickly, and found Mary and Joseph, with the baby lying in a manger. When they saw it, they told many what had been said to them about this child. All who heard it wondered at the things they heard, but Mary kept all these sayings, pondering them in her heart. The shepherds returned, glorifying and praising God because everything they had heard and seen was just as it had been told them.

God announced the Messiah's birth to only one small group of shepherds. In the eyes of both Romans and Jews, the shepherds were nobodies, with no power, no influence, and no importance to justify such an honor. But they were God's choice. Do you think of yourself as too unimportant for God to choose you? Most of the main characters in the Bible were nobodies when God chose them to do something important.

Prayer: Help me remember, Lord, that you connect with people just like me.

Presented at the Temple[9]

When eight days were fulfilled for the circumcision of the child, he was called Jesus, the name given by the angel before he was conceived. In accordance with the Law of Moses, they brought him up to Jerusalem to present him to the Lord as it is written in Exodus, "Every first born son

---

[8] Luke 2:8-20
[9] Luke 2:21-38

shall be called holy to the Lord." They also offered a sacrifice according to what was said in Leviticus, "A pair of turtledoves, or two young pigeons."

At the temple was Simeon, a righteous and devout man living in Jerusalem and looking for the deliverance of Israel. The Holy Spirit was on him and had revealed to him that he would not see death before he had seen the Lord's Christ. Simeon came in the Spirit to the temple just as Jesus was being brought in by his parents. Simeon received the baby into his arms, and blessed God, saying,

"Now you are releasing your servant, Lord,
according to your word, in peace;
for my eyes have seen your salvation,
which you have prepared before the face of all peoples;
a light for revelation to the nations,
and the glory of your people Israel."

Joseph and Mary were marveling at the things he said, and Simeon blessed them, saying to Mary, "This child is set for the falling and rising of many in Israel, and for a sign which is spoken against. Yes, a sword will pierce through your own soul, that the thoughts of many hearts may be revealed."

Also at the temple was Anna, a prophetess, the daughter of Phanuel, of the tribe of Asher. She was of a great age, having lived with a husband for seven years, and as a widow for eighty-four years. Anna was at the temple night and day, worshiping with prayer and fasting. Seeing Jesus, she gave thanks to the Lord, and spoke of him to all those who were looking for redemption in Jerusalem.

Both Simeon and Anna were elderly people who spent much time at the temple, a habit that resulted in them seeing Jesus. Only by being in the right place and seeing the world through eyes of faith could they experience something so extraordinary. How much of your time do you spend in a place where you can see God? Do you have eyes of faith that permit you to see God's presence wherever you are?

Prayer: Put me in the right place and open my eyes, Lord, to see you at work in the world around me.

Visit of the Magi[10]

About this time, Magi from the east came to Jerusalem, saying, "Where is he who is born King of the Jews? We saw his star in the east,

[10] Matthew 2:1-12

and have come to worship him." When King Herod heard this, he was troubled, and all Jerusalem with him. Gathering together the chief priests and scribes, he asked them where the Christ would be born. They said to him, "In Bethlehem of Judea, for this is written through the prophet,

'You Bethlehem, land of Judah,
are in no way least among the
princes of Judah:
for out of you shall come a governor,
who shall shepherd my people,
Israel.'"

Herod secretly called the wise men, and learned from them exactly what time the star appeared. He sent them to Bethlehem, and said, "Go and search diligently for the child. When you have found him, bring me word, so that I also may come and worship him."

The Magi went on their way, and the star, which they had seen in the east, went before them until it came and stood over where the young child was. They rejoiced greatly, and came into the house where they saw the young child with Mary, his mother. They fell down and worshiped him, offering gifts of gold, frankincense, and myrrh. Being warned in a dream not to return to Herod, they went back to their country another way.

The Magi, from an area called Persia in the ancient world and Iran today, were neither wise men nor kings, but astrologers who looked to the stars for insight on what was happening in the world. How remarkable that people from a foreign land and different religion would seek Jesus, while his own people would not. How comfortable are you with people of other religions? Do you see them as part of God's story?

Prayer: Keep me from imagining, Lord, that my grasp of you is always better than anyone whose faith journey is different from mine.

Refugees in Egypt[11]

When the Magi had departed, an angel of the Lord appeared to Joseph in a dream, saying, "Get up and take the young child and his mother, and flee to Egypt. Stay there until I tell you, for Herod will seek the young child to destroy him."

Joseph arose, took his family by night, and left for Egypt. They lived there until the death of Herod, fulfilling what was spoken by the Lord through the prophet: "Out of Egypt I called my son."

When Herod realized the Magi didn't do as told, he was filled with rage, and ordered the death of all boys two years old and under in

---

[11] Matthew 2:13-23; Luke 2:39-40

Bethlehem and the surrounding countryside, according to the exact time he had learned from the Magi. Then what was spoken by Jeremiah the prophet was fulfilled:

"A voice was heard in Ramah,
lamentation, weeping and great mourning,
Rachel weeping for her children;
she wouldn't be comforted,
because they were no more."

Herod's lust for power was so great he had no hesitation to murder innocent children to destroy a potential rival. Herod maintained his power through ruthless suppression of dissent. What examples come to mind concerning ruthless actions taken today to gain or preserve power? Could you ever be corrupted by power?

Prayer: Help me, Lord, never become so addicted to power and privilege that I would harm others to hold on it.

After Herod died, an angel of the Lord appeared in a dream to Joseph in Egypt, saying, "Arise and take the young child and his mother, and go into the land of Israel, for those who sought his life are dead."

He arose, took the boy and his mother, and came into the land of Israel. When he heard Archelaus was reigning over Judea in the place of his father, Herod, he was afraid to go there. Being warned in a dream, he withdrew into the region of Galilee, and came to live in Nazareth. This fulfilled what was spoken through the prophets: "He will be called a Nazarene."

The child grew, and became strong in spirit and filled with wisdom as the grace of God was upon him.

My Father's House[12]

When Jesus was twelve years old, he went with his parents to Jerusalem to celebrate Passover as was their custom. After the feast, Jesus stayed behind without Joseph and Mary's awareness. Supposing him to be with others in the group, they went a day's journey, and looked for him among their relatives and friends. When they didn't find him, they returned to Jerusalem.

After three days they found him in the temple, sitting in the middle of the teachers, listening to them, and asking questions. All who heard him were amazed at his understanding and his answers.

When his parents found him, they were astonished, and his mother said to him, "Son, why have you treated us this way? Your father and I

[12] Luke 2:41-52

were anxiously looking for you."

He said to them, "Why were you looking for me? Didn't you know I must be in my Father's house?" They didn't understand the meaning of what he said to them. Back home in Nazareth, he was subject to his parents, and his mother kept all these sayings in her heart. Jesus increased in wisdom and stature, and in favor with God and everyone.

Contrary to what many imagine, this is not a story of Jesus as a 12-year-old boy teaching scholars in the temple. What people were most impressed with were the questions he asked. Sometimes a good question is as important as a good answer. How have your questions about God been handled by others? Were you taken seriously, or were you dismissed, criticized, or given simplistic answers?

Prayer: Give me wisdom, Lord, in facing my own questions and those of others.

Chapter 2: Preparations

John the Baptizer[13]

In the fifteenth year of the reign of Tiberius Caesar, the word of God came to John, the son of Zechariah, in the wilderness. He came into the region around the Jordan, preaching a baptism of repentance for the remission of sins. As it is written in the book of Isaiah the prophet,

"The voice of one crying in the wilderness,
'Make ready the way of the Lord.
Make his paths straight.
Every valley will be filled.
Every mountain and hill will be brought low.
The crooked will become straight,
and the rough ways smooth.
All flesh will see God's salvation.'"

John wore clothing made of camel's hair, with a leather belt around his waist. His food was locusts and wild honey. People from Jerusalem, Judea, and all the region around the Jordan went out to him. They were baptized by him in the Jordan, confessing their sins.

For centuries, Hebrew prophets had been saying a day would come when everything wrong in the world would be made right as violence, injustice and suffering gave way to peace and well-being. John told people to get ready because these ancient prophecies were about to come true. What troubles you most about the world today? Can you imagine a world of peace and well-being? Wouldn't its arrival be incredible news?

Prayer: Help me be like John the Baptizer, Lord, pointing people to your kingdom of peace and well-being.

This is what John said, when the Jews sent priests and Levites from Jerusalem to ask him, "Who are you?"

He declared, "I am not the Christ."

---

[13] Matthew 3:1-6; Mark 1:2-6; Luke 3:1-6; John 1:19-23

They said, "What then? Are you Elijah?"

He replied, "I am not."

"Are you the prophet?"

He answered, "No."

They said therefore to him, "Who are you? Give us an answer to take back to those who sent us. What do you say about yourself?"

He said, "I am the voice of one crying in the wilderness, 'Make straight the way of the Lord,' as Isaiah the prophet said."

The Message of John the Baptizer[14]

When he saw a number of Pharisees and Sadducees coming to be baptized, he said to them, "You brood of vipers, who warned you to flee from the wrath to come? Produce fruit worthy of repentance! Don't think to yourselves, 'We have Abraham for our father.' I tell you God is able to raise up children to Abraham from these stones. Even now the ax lies at the root of the trees. Every tree that doesn't produce good fruit is cut down, and cast into the fire."

The crowds asked him, "What then must we do?"

He answered them, "Whoever has two coats, give to the one who has none. Whoever has food, do the same."

Tax collectors also came to be baptized, and they asked, "Teacher, what must we do?"

He said to them, "Collect no more than what is appointed to you."

Soldiers also asked him, "What about us? What must we do?"

He said to them, "Extort from no one by violence, neither accuse anyone wrongfully. Be content with your wages."

Repentance is not about feeling sorry, but about changing direction. John didn't tell people to get ready for what God was about to do by becoming more religious. His message focused on daily life: act with compassion and generosity; live with honor and integrity. Many today think our country is headed in the wrong direction. Do you think a practical message like John's could get our nation on track? Is your life on the right path?

Prayer: Turn me around, Lord, when the direction I'm headed is wrong.

As everyone was excited, and wondered whether John was the Christ, he told them, "I baptize you with water, but one comes who is mightier than I, the strap of whose sandals I am not worthy to loosen. He will baptize you in the Holy Spirit and fire. His fan is in his hand, and he

[14] Matthew 3:7-12; Mark 1:7-8; Luke 3:7-18; John 1:24-28

will thoroughly cleanse the threshing floor, and will gather the wheat into his barn; but he will burn up the chaff with unquenchable fire."

Then with many other exhortations he preached good news to the people.

The Baptism of Jesus[15]

Jesus came from Galilee to be baptized by John, but John questioned him: "I need to be baptized by you, and you come to me?"

Jesus, answered, "Allow it for now; this is the fitting way for us to fulfill all righteousness."

When Jesus was baptized, he came out of the water, and the heavens opened before him. He saw the Spirit of God descending as a dove, and resting on him. A voice from heaven said, "You are my beloved Son; with you I am well pleased."

The next day, John saw Jesus coming to him, and said, "Behold, the Lamb of God, who takes away the sin of the world! This is the one of whom I said, 'After me comes a man who is above me, because he existed before me.' I didn't know who he was, but I came baptizing in water to reveal him to Israel." John testified, "I have seen the Spirit descending like a dove, and remaining on him. I didn't recognize him, but the one who sent me to baptize in water, said to me, 'On whoever you see the Spirit descending and remaining, the same is the one who baptizes in the Holy Spirit.' I have seen and have testified that this is the Son of God."

Jesus was both known and unknown to John. He saw Jesus as a good man who didn't need to be baptized to signify the forgiveness of his sins. He hadn't yet grasped, though, that Jesus was far more than a good man. At his baptism, Jesus was touched by God's Spirit and affirmed in God's love. Have you been baptized? Was it for you an experience of the presence of God's Spirit and the depth of God's love?

Prayer: Help me experience, Lord, the joy of being filled with your Spirit and your love.

Tested in the Wilderness[16]

Jesus, full of the Holy Spirit, was led by the Spirit into the wilderness to be tempted by the devil. When he had fasted forty days and nights, he was hungry. The tempter came and said to him, "If you are the Son of God, command these stones to become bread."

---

[15] Matthew 3:13-17; Mark 1:9-11; Luke 3:21-22; John 1:29-34

[16] Matthew 4:1-11; Mark 1:12-13; Luke 4:1-13

But he answered, "It is written, 'Man shall not live by bread alone, but by every word that comes from the mouth of God.'"

Then the devil took him into the holy city. He set him on the pinnacle of the temple, and said to him, "If you are the Son of God, throw yourself down, for it is written, 'He will put his angels in charge of you.' and, 'On their hands they will bear you up, so you don't dash your foot against a stone.'"

Jesus said to him, "Again, it is written, 'You shall not test the Lord, your God.'"

The devil took him to an exceedingly high mountain, and showed him all the kingdoms of the world. He said to him, "I will give you all their power and glory, for it has been given to me, and I can give it to whoever I want. If you will worship me, it will all be yours."

Then Jesus said to him, "Get behind me, Satan! For it is written, 'You shall worship the Lord your God, and you shall serve him only.'"

Then the devil left him until an opportune time, and angels came to his aid.

As is true throughout the gospels, the devil in this story is present, but not in charge. Jesus is led by the Spirit to a testing that will demonstrate his faithfulness to God. The situation is much like that of Adam and Eve in the Garden of Eden with one big difference: this time Jesus prevailed and the devil struck out. The temptations here weren't unique to Jesus: use your resources for yourself; make God prove his love; compromise to gain power and privilege. What have been some of your own persistent temptations? Do you find it difficult to be faithful?

Prayer: When I am tempted to follow the easy path, Lord, give me the courage and wisdom to be faithful to you.

The Genealogy of Jesus[17]

Jesus was about thirty years of age when he began his ministry, being the son (as was supposed) of Joseph. Among his ancestors were: David, Abraham, and a host of other illustrious men, plus four notable women:

- **Tamar** – who tricked her father-in-law into making her pregnant (Genesis 38)

Genealogies are usually of little interest outside the family. This might also be true for the genealogy of Jesus were it not for the inclusion of four highly unusual women. Is ancestry important to you? Are you ashamed of infamous ancestors or proud of distinguished ones?

Prayer: Help me remember, Lord, the only ancestry that matters is being your child, made in your image.

---

[17] Matt 1:1-17; Luke 3:23-38

- **Rahab** – a prostitute who lied to protect the Hebrew spies prior to the defeat of Jericho (Joshua 2)
- **Ruth** – a woman of the Moabites, a hated nation whose people were excluded from contact with Israelites (Ruth 1)
- **Bathsheba** – a woman made pregnant by David in an adulterous affair (or rape) that led to her husband's murder (2 Samuel 2)

The First Followers[18]

Sometime later, as John was standing with two of his disciples, he saw Jesus walking by and said, "Look, the Lamb of God!" The disciples heard what he said and began to follow Jesus, who turned and seeing them, said, "What are you looking for?"

They said to him, "Teacher, where are you staying?"

He said to them, "Come, and see."

It was about 4 p.m. They came and saw where he was staying, and spent the rest of the day there. One of the two who heard John, and followed was Andrew, who found his brother, Simon, and said to him, "We have found the Christ!" He brought him to Jesus, who looked at him, and said, "You are Simon, the son of Jonah. You shall be called Peter."

On the next day, Jesus went into Galilee and found Philip. Jesus said to him, "Follow me." Now Philip was from Bethsaida, of the city of Andrew and Peter. Philip found Nathanael, and said to him, "We have found the one spoken of in the prophets and by Moses in the law: Jesus of Nazareth, the son of Joseph."

Nathanael said to him, "Can any good thing come out of Nazareth?"

Philip said to him, "Come and see."

Jesus saw Nathanael coming to him, and said, "Look: an Israelite in whom there is no deceit!"

Nathanael said to him, "How do you know me?"

Jesus answered him, "Before Philip called you, I saw you when you were under the fig tree."

There is something so inviting about Jesus' words, "Come and see." There is no sense of pressure or obligation, no guilt or manipulation, no inducement through hype and promises; it was just a simple, "Come and see." Philip used the same phrase with Nathanael. Were you invited to discover Jesus this way? Have you ever invited someone else to do the same?

Prayer: Keep reminding me, Lord: people come to you by invitation, not by heavy-handed persuasion.

[18] John 1:35-51

Nathanael answered him, "Rabbi, you are the Son of God, the King of Israel!"

Jesus answered him, "Do you believe because I said I saw you underneath the fig tree? You will see greater things than this! One day you will see heaven opened, and the angels of God going up and coming down to the Son of Man."

Turning Water into Wine[19]

Three days later, there was a wedding in Cana of Galilee. Jesus' mother was there, along with Jesus and his disciples. When the wine ran out, Jesus' mother said to him, "They have no wine."

Jesus said to her, "Woman, what does that have to do with you and me? My hour has not yet come."

His mother said to the servants, "Whatever he says to you, do it." Now there were six water pots of stone set there for Jewish ceremonial cleansing, containing twenty or thirty gallons apiece. Jesus said, "Fill the water pots with water." They filled them up to the brim. Then he said, "Now draw some out, and take it to the ruler of the feast."

When the ruler of the feast tasted the water now become wine, and didn't know where it came from (only the servants who had drawn the water knew), the ruler of the feast called the bridegroom, and said to him, "Everyone serves the good wine first, and when the guests have drunk freely, they serve what is worse. But you have kept the good wine until now!"

This was the first of the signs Jesus did in Cana of Galilee. It revealed his glory, and his disciples believed in him.

This transformation from water to wine was a sign, not a magic trick. Just as the dry, emptiness of old water jars was replaced by water and then by the wine, so would the old way of seeking to please God by strict obedience to endless rules be replaced by new life coming from the indwelling of the Holy Spirit. Has your experience of church included both dryness and vitality? Can you give an example of each?

Prayer: Thank you, Lord, for giving me new life and hope. Show me someone I can invite into this same experience

---

[19] John 2:1-11

Chapter 3: Early Ministry

Cleansing the Temple[20]

After this, he went down to Capernaum, along with his mother, his brothers, and his disciples; they stayed there a few days. When the Jewish Passover was at hand, Jesus went up to Jerusalem.

He found in the temple those who sold oxen, sheep, and doves, and those who exchanged Roman coins for Jewish ones. He made a whip of cords, and drove the animals out of the temple. Then he poured out the changers' money, and turned over their tables. To those who sold doves, he said, "Take these things out of here! Don't make my Father's house a marketplace!" His disciples remembered that it was written, "Zeal for your house will consume me."

The original idea of sacrifices was that offerings to God should represent the best of what people had. As time went by, people were told this wasn't good enough: only what was bought in the temple was worthy of being sacrificed in the temple. Corruption ran rampant. Are there people today who profit unethically from people's sincere desire to connect with God? Is there a need to "clean house" in today's church?

Prayer: Create in me a zeal, Lord, to confront those who take advantage of the most vulnerable.

The Jews therefore asked him, "What sign do you show us to prove your authority to do these things?"

Jesus answered, "Destroy this temple, and in three days I will raise it up."

The Jews said, "It took forty-six years to build this temple! Will you raise it up in three days?" But he spoke of the temple of his body. When he was raised from the dead, his disciples remembered this, and believed what Jesus had said.

While he was in Jerusalem at the Passover, many believed in his

---

[20] John 2:11-25

name when they saw what he did. Jesus didn't trust himself to them, however, because he knew human nature; no one had to tell him what people were like.

Talking with Nicodemus[21]

A Pharisee named Nicodemus, a ruler of the Jews, came to Jesus by night and said, "Rabbi, we know you are a teacher come from God, for no one can do the signs you do, unless God is with him."

Jesus answered him, "Unless you are born again, you will never see God's kingdom."

Nicodemus said to him, "How can a man be born when he is old? Can he enter a second time into his mother's womb?"

Jesus answered, "Unless you are born of water and spirit, you can't enter into God's kingdom! What is born of the flesh is flesh; what is born of the Spirit is spirit. Don't marvel that I say, 'You must be born again.' The wind blows where it wants to, and you hear its sound, but don't know where it comes from or where it goes. So is everyone who is born of the Spirit."

Nicodemus answered him, "How can this be?"

Words are often ambiguous. Jesus speaks here of being born from above or being born again; Nicodemus assumes it is the latter and is confused. Jesus makes clear, though, the Holy Spirit's role in this: becoming a child of God is never mechanical or formulaic. Has there been a clear and memorable moment of a new birth like this in your spiritual journey? If not, how would you describe your journey?

Prayer: Help me remember, Lord: people become believers, not because we persuade them, but because you draw them to yourself.

Jesus answered him, "You are a teacher of Israel, and don't understand these things? We speak what we know, and tell what we have seen, yet you don't receive our witness. If I tell you earthly things and you don't believe, how will you believe if I tell you heavenly things? No one has gone into heaven except the Son of Man who came from there.

As Moses lifted up the serpent in the wilderness, even so the Son of Man must be lifted up, that everyone who believes in him should have eternal life. God so loved the world that he gave his one and only Son, that whoever believes in him should not perish, but have eternal life. For God didn't send his Son into the world to condemn the world, but that the world should be saved through him. Whoever believes in him is not

21 John 3:1-21

judged. Whoever doesn't believe has been judged already, by not believing in the name of the one and only Son of God.

This is the judgment, that light has come into the world, and people loved darkness rather than light, for their works were evil. Those who do evil hate the light, and don't come to it, to keep their works hidden. Those who do the truth come to the light, that their works may be revealed as being done in God."

John's View of Jesus[22]

Jesus went with his disciples into the land of Judea, staying with them, and baptizing. John, who had not yet been thrown into prison, was also baptizing in that area because of the ample water.

There arose a question on the part of John's disciples with some Jews about purification. They brought their question to John, and also a complaint: "Rabbi, the one you told us about who was with you beyond the Jordan is baptizing, and everyone is going to him."

John answered, "People can receive nothing, unless it has been given them from heaven. You know I said, 'I am not the Christ,' but, 'I have been sent before him.' The one who welcomes the bride is the bridegroom; the friend of the bridegroom, who stands and hears him, rejoices greatly at his coming. This is my joy, and it is now made full.

He must increase, but I must decrease. He who comes from above is above all. Anyone from the earth belongs to the earth, and speaks of the earth. He who comes from heaven is above all. He speaks of what he has seen and heard, and no one receives his message. Anyone who has received his message, though, verifies the truthfulness of God. The one God has sent speaks the words of God because God gives him the Spirit without limit. The Father loves the Son, and has given all things into his hand. Those who believe in the Son have eternal life, but

John preached a baptism of repentance to those whose lives were headed in the wrong direction, but his disciples were still caught up in the ways of the world. They were jealous of the attention Jesus received, while John delighted in it. Do you rejoice in the success of others or find yourself envious? Has jealousy ever been a problem in your relationships?

Prayer: Help me focus on what you've given me, Lord, not on what others have.

[22] John 3:22-36

those who disobey the Son won't see life because the wrath of God remains on them."

The Woman at the Well[23]

When Jesus learned the Pharisees had heard he was making and baptizing more disciples than John (though Jesus himself didn't baptize, but his disciples did), he left Judea, passing through Samaria on his way to Galilee. He came to Sychar, a city of Samaria near the land Jacob had given to his son, Joseph. Jacob's well was there, and Jesus, tired from his journey, sat down by it. In the middle of the day, a woman of Samaria came to draw water. Jesus, whose disciples had gone into the city to buy food, said to her, "Give me a drink."

The woman replied, "How is it that you, a Jew, ask for a drink from me, a Samaritan woman?" (Jews have no dealings with Samaritans.)

Jesus said, "If you knew the gift of God, and who it is who said, 'Give me a drink,' you would have asked him, and he would have given you living water."

The woman said, "Sir, you have nothing to draw with, and the well is deep. Where do you get that living water? Are you greater than our father, Jacob, who gave us the well, and drank of it himself, as did his children, and his livestock?"

Jesus answered her, "Everyone who drinks of this water will thirst again, but whoever drinks of the water I give will never thirst again; the water I give will become a well of water springing up to eternal life."

The woman said to him, "Sir, give me this water, so that I don't get thirsty, and have to keep coming all the way here."

Jesus said to her, "Go, call your husband to come here."

The woman answered, "I have no husband."

Jesus said to her, "You said well, 'I have no husband,' for you have had five husbands; and the one you now have is not your husband. You have spoken truly."

The disastrous marital history of the woman was probably not much of a secret: only a social outcast would go to the well for water in the hottest part of the day. Nevertheless, the woman was amazed Jesus knew so much about her. How much of your life is secret? Is it scary to think that God knows all, or amazing to think that God knows all and still loves you?

Prayer: Let me never forget, Lord, there are no secrets I can hide from you.

[23] John 4:1-29

The woman said to him, "I see you are a prophet. Our fathers worshiped on this mountain, and you Jews say Jerusalem is the place for people to worship."

Jesus said to her, "Believe me, the hour comes, when neither in this mountain, nor in Jerusalem, will you worship the Father. You worship what you don't know. We worship what we know, for salvation is from the Jews. But the hour is coming and already here, when the true worshipers will worship the Father in spirit and truth, for the Father seeks such to be his worshipers. God is spirit, and those who worship him must worship in spirit and truth."

The woman said to him, "I know the Messiah will come, he who is called the Christ. When he comes, he will declare to us all things."

Jesus said to her, "I am he, the one who speaks to you."

At this, his disciples came. They marveled that he was speaking with a woman, yet no one said, "What are you looking for?" or, "Why do you speak with her?" The woman left her water pot, went into the city, and said to the people, "Come and see a man who told me everything I ever did. Can this be the Christ?"

Fields Ripe for Harvest[24]

Many went out of the city, and were coming to him. In the meanwhile, the disciples urged him, saying, "Rabbi, eat."

But he said to them, "I have food to eat that you don't know about."

The disciples said to each other, "Has anyone brought him something to eat?"

Jesus said to them, "My food is to do the will of him who sent me, and to accomplish his work. Don't you say, 'There are yet four months until the harvest?' I tell you, lift up your eyes, and look at the fields: they are white for harvest already. Those who reap receive wages, and gather fruit to eternal life; those who sow and those who reap rejoice together. For in this the saying is true, 'One sows, and another reaps.' I

The physical needs Jesus had were real, but not dominant. He was tired and stopped to rest. He was thirsty and asked for water. He was hungry, but found his nourishment in doing God's will. Do you control your appetites or do your appetites control you? Are you honest about the addictions or obsessions you have?

Prayer: Give me strength, Lord, to control the desires that seek to control me.

[24] John 4:30-42

sent you to reap that for which you haven't labored. Others have labored, and you have benefited from their labor."

From that city many of the Samaritans believed in him because of the word of the woman who said, "He told me everything I ever did." When the Samaritans came to him, they begged him to stay with them and he stayed there two days. Many more believed because of his word. They said to the woman, "Now we believe, not because of your speaking; for we have heard for ourselves, and know that this is indeed the Christ, the Savior of the world."

Preaching at Nazareth[25]

He came to Nazareth, where he had been brought up. He went, as was his custom, to the synagogue on the Sabbath, and stood up to read. The book of Isaiah the prophet was handed to him. He opened the book and found the place where it was written,

"The Spirit of the Lord is on me,
because he has anointed me to preach good news to the poor.
He has sent me to heal the broken hearted,
to proclaim release to the captives,
recovering of sight to the blind,
to deliver those who are crushed,
and to proclaim the acceptable
year of the Lord."

He closed the book, gave it back to the attendant, and sat down. The eyes of all in the synagogue were fastened on him as he began, "Today, this Scripture has been fulfilled in your hearing."

All talked about him, and wondered at the gracious words he spoke. "Where did this man get this wisdom, and these mighty works? Isn't this the carpenter's son? Isn't Mary his mother, and James, Joses, Simon, and Judas his brothers? Aren't all of his sisters with us? Where

The people at Nazareth were upset Jesus didn't do the miracles in his hometown that he did elsewhere. They were even more upset when he said God at times showed more compassion to foreigners than to Jews. How do you feel about immigrants and refugees coming to the United States? Do you resent resources being used to meet their needs when so many Americans are in need as well, or do you see them as neighbors to love?

Prayer: Change my mind, Lord, when I start thinking like the people who rose up against Jesus.

25 Mark 6:1-6; Luke 4:16-30

then did this man come up with all of these things?" And they were offended by him.

Jesus said, "Doubtless you will tell me this parable, 'Physician, heal yourself! Whatever we have heard done at Capernaum, do also here in your hometown.' I tell you no prophet is respected in his hometown. There were many widows in Israel in the days of Elijah, when there was no rain for three years and six months, and a great famine came over all the land, but Elijah was sent to none of them, except to Zarephath, in the land of Sidon, to a widow. There were also many lepers in Israel in the time of Elisha the prophet, yet not one of them was cleansed, except Naaman, the Syrian."

Everyone in the synagogue was enraged as they heard these things. They rose up, and took him out of the city to throw him off the cliff on which their city was built. But passing through the middle of them, he left town.

Living in Capernaum[26]

Leaving Nazareth, he came and lived in Capernaum, which is by the sea, in the region of Zebulun and Naphtali, that what was spoken through Isaiah the prophet might be fulfilled:

"The land of Zebulun and the land of Naphtali,
toward the sea, beyond the Jordan,
Galilee of the Gentiles,
the people who sat in darkness saw a great light,
to those who sat in the region and shadow of death,
to them light has dawned."

Jesus began to preach, saying, "Repent! For the kingdom of God is at hand; repent and believe the good news."

Biblical prophecy is rarely a simple matter of predictions coming true. Sometimes they come true in ways only understood later because what happens looks different than what was expected. Have you ever seen evidence of God doing something good in your life when looking back on it, but not at all while it was happening?

Prayer: Open the eyes of my heart, Lord, to recognize your presence when things turn out different than I wanted.

Catching Fish[27]

The report about him went out into all Syria. They brought to him

[26] Matthew 4:12-17; Mark 1:14-15; Luke 4:14-15; John 4:43-46
[27] Matthew 4:18-25; Mark 1:16-20; Mark 3:7-12; Luke 5:1-11

epileptics, paralytics, and all who were afflicted with various diseases or possessed with evil spirits, and he healed them. Great crowds from Galilee, Decapolis, Jerusalem, Judea and from beyond the Jordan followed him.

He had healed many and everyone wanted to touch him; he told his disciples a little boat should be nearby to keep the crowd from crushing him. When unclean spirits saw him, they fell down before him and cried, "You are the Son of God!" He sternly warned them not to make him known.

One day, when people gathered to hear the word of God, Jesus was standing by the Sea of Galilee. He saw two boats on the edge of the water, but the fishermen had left them, and were washing their nets. He entered into Simon's boat, and asked him to put out a little from the land. He sat down and taught the multitudes from the boat. When he had finished speaking, he said to Simon, "Put out into the deep, and let down your nets for a catch."

Simon answered him, "Master, we worked all night, and took nothing; but at your word I will let down the net." When they had done this, they caught a great multitude of fish, and their net was breaking. They signaled to their partners in the other boat to come and help them. They filled both boats to the point of sinking. Simon Peter, when he saw it, fell down at Jesus' knees, saying, "Depart from me, Lord, for I am a sinful man." He was amazed, and all who were with him, at the amount of fish they had caught; so also were James and John, sons of Zebedee, who were partners with Simon.

Jesus said to Simon, "Don't be afraid. From now on you'll be catching people."

These disciples made their living by fishing. A huge catch of fish like this meant a big payday; Peter may have felt unworthy to receive something for which he hadn't worked. Or maybe he just felt guilty about his lack of faith. Would you have reacted similarly in Peter's situation? When something wonderful happens to you, are you more likely to feel grateful about it or anxious that something bad might be coming next?

Prayer: Don't let my feelings of unworthiness, Lord, keep me from experiencing your gracious gifts.

Authority over Illness[28]

Jesus came down to Capernaum, and was teaching on the Sabbath. People were astonished at his teaching and the authority with which he

[28] Mark 1:21-34; Luke 4:31-41

spoke. In the synagogue, a man with an unclean spirit, cried out, "What have we to do with you, Jesus of Nazareth? Have you come to destroy us? I know you who you are: the Holy One of God!"

Jesus rebuked him, saying, "Be silent, and come out of him!" When the evil spirit had thrown the man down in their midst, he came out, having done him no harm.

Everyone was amazed, and said to one another, "What is this? With authority and power he commands the unclean spirits, and they come out!" News about him went out into every place of the surrounding region.

He rose up from the synagogue, and entered into Simon's house. Simon's mother-in-law was ill with a high fever, and they begged him to help her. He stood over her, took her by the hand, lifted her up and rebuked the fever. It left her, and she rose up and served them.

At evening, when the sun had set, they brought to him all who were sick, and those who were possessed by evil spirits. All the city was gathered together at the door. He healed many who were sick with various diseases, and cast out many evil spirits. He didn't allow the evil spirits to speak, because they knew him.

We know our bodies and minds have great ability within limits and over time to heal themselves. What is pictured here, though, is Jesus speaking with authority to fevers and spirits, and people being made whole in an instant. The way this happens isn't magic, but it is mystery. Do you approach stories such as these with faith or skepticism? What experiences in your life have shaped your approach?

Prayer: Open the eyes of my heart and mind, Lord, to all of life's mysteries.

The Urgency of Following Jesus[29]

Early in the morning, while it was still dark, Jesus rose up and went out to a deserted place, and prayed. Simon and those who were with him followed him. When they found him, they said, "Everyone is looking for you."

Jesus said, "Let's go to the next towns that I may preach there also, because I came for this reason."

As they went on the way, a man said to him, "I want to follow you wherever you go, Lord."

Jesus said to him, "The foxes have holes, and the birds of the sky have nests, but the Son of Man has no place to lay his head."

[29] Matthew 4:23-25; 8:14-22; Mark 1:35-39; Luke 4:42-44; Luke 9:57-62

Jesus said to another, "Follow me!" But he said, "Lord, allow me first to go and bury my father." Jesus said to him, "Leave the dead to bury the dead; you go and announce God's kingdom."

Another said, "I want to follow you, Lord, but first allow me to say good-bye to those who are at my house." Jesus said to him, "No one, having put his hand to the plow, and looking back, is fit for God's kingdom."

Few people who met Jesus were able to go back unchanged to the life they had always known. His message was both inviting and challenging; timid, half-hearted responses wouldn't do. Does the urgency and priority of Jesus' call speak to your own experience of faith? Do you have obstacles in your life which make it difficult to follow Jesus fully?

Prayer: Give me the courage I need, Lord, to respond fully to your call.

Cleansing a Leper[30]

Jesus went about in all Galilee, teaching in synagogues, preaching the good news of the kingdom, and healing every disease and sickness among the people.

While he was in one of the cities, a man full of leprosy came to him, kneeling down and saying, "If you want to, you can make me clean."

Moved with compassion, Jesus stretched out his hand and touched him, saying, "I do want to. Be made clean." When he had said this, the leprosy departed, and he was made clean. Jesus strictly warned him, "Say nothing to anyone, but go show yourself to the priest, and offer for your cleansing the things which Moses commanded, as a testimony to them."

But the man went out, and began to proclaim it everywhere, so that Jesus could no more openly enter a city, but stayed in desert places; and still they came to him from everywhere.

By touching a leper, Jesus did something unheard of for people in his day. Rather than being contaminated by the contact, however, his own contagious wholeness flowed to the leper, curing and cleansing him. Who are the untouchables in our world today? Is it possible for them to be made whole by the touch of those who care?

Prayer: Make the wholeness in me, Lord, stronger than the brokenness in those who feel untouchable.

Healing a Paralytic[31]

When Jesus came again to Capernaum after some days, people heard

30 Matthew 8:1-4; Mark 1:40-45; Luke 5:12-16

31 Matthew 9:1-8; Mark 2:1-12; Luke 5:17-26

he was in town. People gathered at the house until there was no more room, not even around the door, and he taught them. Four people came, carrying a paralytic. When they could not come inside, they made a hole in the roof, and let down the mat a paralytic was lying on. Seeing their faith, Jesus said to the paralytic, "Son, your sins are forgiven."

Some of the scribes sitting there were saying in their hearts, "Why does this man speak such blasphemies? Who can forgive sins but God alone?"

Jesus knew what they were thinking, and said to them, "Why do you think these things in your hearts? Which is easier, to tell the paralytic, 'Your sins are forgiven;' or to say, 'Arise, take up your bed, and walk?' But that you may know the Son of Man has authority on earth to forgive sins"— he said to the paralytic— "I tell you, arise, take up your mat, and go to your house."

He arose, and took up his mat, and went out in front of them all; the crowd was amazed, and glorified God, saying, "We have never seen anything like this!"

We don't know much about this man except that he had a home, a bed, a disability, and four great friends! Everything in this story begins when Jesus sees the faith of these friends. Do you have friends who would act on your behalf like those in this story? Are you a friend like that to others?

Prayer: Show me what to do, Lord, when my friends are in need of help.

Calling a Tax Collector[32]

He went out again by the seaside, where a crowd came to him, and he taught them. As he passed by, he saw Levi, the son of Alphaeus, sitting at the tax office, and said to him, "Follow me." And Levi got up and followed him.

Jesus was reclining at the table in Levi's house, and many tax collectors and sinners sat down with him and his disciples. The scribes and the Pharisees, when they saw what Jesus was doing, said to his disciples, "Why is it that he

---

Tax collectors were perhaps the most despised people in Israel, considered crooks and traitors by everyone. There could hardly have been a less likely person for Jesus to invite to follow him. Who are the despised people in our own world we would likely vote "least likely to follow Jesus?"

Prayer: Help me grasp, Lord, that no one is beyond the reach of your love.

---

[32] Matthew 9:9-13; Mark 2:13-17; Luke 5:27-32

eats and drinks with tax collectors and sinners?"

When Jesus heard this, he said to them, "Those who are healthy have no need of a physician, but only those who are sick. I came not to call the righteous, but sinners to repentance."

Old and New Wineskins[33]

Someone said to him, "Why do John's disciples frequently fast and pray like the disciples of the Pharisees, but yours eat and drink?"

He said to them, "Can you make the friends of the bridegroom fast, while the bridegroom is with them? The days will come when the bridegroom will be taken away from them; they will fast in those days."

He also told a parable to them. "No one puts a piece from a new garment on an old garment, or else he will tear the new; also the piece from the new will not match the old. No one puts new wine into old wine skins, or else the new wine will burst the skins, and it will be spilled, and the skins will be destroyed. But new wine must be put into fresh wine skins, and both are preserved. And no one having drunk old wine soon desires new, but says instead, 'The old is better.'"

As leather wineskins age, they become less flexible. New wine, as it continues to ferment, expands and stretches the skin. If the skins are too brittle, they rupture and the wine is lost. Jesus was speaking here of religious traditions. What new ideas or new people are most likely to create tension in churches? What can be done to help old and new work together?

Prayer: Help me treat with dignity and respect, Lord, those whose ideas and traditions are different from my own.

Observing the Sabbath[34]

Jesus was walking on a Sabbath day through the grain fields, and his disciples began, as they walked along, to pluck the ears of grain. The Pharisees said to him, "Why do they do what is not lawful on the Sabbath?"

He said to them, "Did you never read what David did, when he had need, and was hungry? He entered into God's house, and ate the sacred bread, which is not lawful to eat except for the priests, and gave also to those who were with him?" He said to them, "The Sabbath was made for man, not man for the Sabbath. The Son of Man is lord even of the Sabbath."

33 Matthew 9:14-17; Mark 2:18-22; Luke 5:33-39
34 Matthew 12:1-14; Mark 2:23-3:6; Luke 6:1-11

On another Sabbath Jesus entered the synagogue and taught. There was a man with a withered right hand, and the scribes and Pharisees watched to see if Jesus would heal him on the Sabbath, and they could accuse him. Jesus knew their thoughts, and said to the man, "Rise up, and stand in the middle." Then Jesus said to them, "I will ask you something: Is it lawful on the Sabbath to do good, or to do harm? To save a life, or to kill?" He looked around at them all with anger, grieved at their hardness of heart, and said to the man, "Stretch out your hand." He did, and his hand was restored as sound as the other. They were filled with rage, and talked with one another about what they might do to Jesus.

One of the Ten Commandments is to honor the Sabbath, the last day of the week, as a day of rest. In Jesus' day, this had become an obsession about refraining from everything lest it be called work. Jesus said people had missed the point entirely: a day of rest was a gift of God, not a burden. Do you observe a day of rest or are you more likely to feel guilty if you're not doing something productive? What do you find most restful? What feeds your soul?

Prayer: Slow me down, Lord, to find the peace and rest you created me to have.

Choosing the Twelve[35]

Jesus withdrew from there, and great crowds followed him. He healed them all, and told them not to make him known. This fulfilled what was spoken through Isaiah the prophet:

"Behold, my servant whom I have chosen;
  my beloved in whom my soul is well pleased:
I will put my Spirit on him.
  He will proclaim justice to the nations.
He will not strive, nor shout;
  neither will anyone hear his voice in the streets.
He won't break a bruised reed.
  He won't quench a smoking flax,
until he leads justice to victory.
  In his name, the nations will hope."

Jesus went out to the mountain to pray, and continued all night in prayer. When it was day, he called his disciples, and from them chose twelve apostles to be with him, and to be sent out to preach and have authority to cast out evil spirits: Simon Peter; his brother, Andrew;

[35] Matthew 12:15-21; Mark 3:13-19; Luke 6:12-16

James; John; Philip; Bartholomew; Matthew; Thomas; James, the son of Alphaeus; Simon, who was called the Zealot; Judas the son of James; and Judas Iscariot, who became a traitor.

Multitudes followed Jesus, but twelve were chosen to symbolize the historic tribes of Israel. Before deciding who would be among the twelve, Jesus spent a night in prayer. How much time do you spend in prayer or meditation? Are your prayers typically lists of what you want God to do for you? Do you ever spend time being quiet, opening your heart and mind to God?

Prayer: Thank you, Lord, for inviting me to spend time with you and listen for your voice.

Chapter 4: The Sermon on the Mount

The Beatitudes[36]

Seeing the crowd which had gathered, Jesus went up onto a mountain and sat down. His followers came to him, and he taught them, saying,

Jesus taught about the Kingdom of God, in which God's will is done fully and completely "on earth as it is in heaven." Such a world is very different from the world we know. Those who are pitied in this world, for instance, are described by Jesus as the ones who are blessed in God's kingdom. In what ways do you feel fortunate or unfortunate? Is your evaluation of your life based on the world's values or God's?

Prayer: Give me a clear perspective, Lord, on what in life really matters.

Blessed are the poor in spirit,
for theirs is the kingdom of God.
Blessed are those who mourn,
for they shall be comforted.
Blessed are the meek,
for they shall inherit the earth.
Blessed are those who hunger and thirst for righteousness,
for they shall be filled.
Blessed are the merciful,
for they shall obtain mercy.
Blessed are the pure in heart,
for they shall see God.
Blessed are the peacemakers,
for they shall be called children of God.
Blessed are those who have been persecuted for righteousness' sake,
for theirs is the kingdom of God.

---

[36] Matthew 5:1-10

Salt and Light[37]

"You are the salt of the earth. If the salt has lost its flavor, with what will it be restored? It is then good for nothing, but to be cast out and walked on. You are the light of the world. A city on a hill can't be hidden. Neither do you light a lamp, and put it under a basket, but on a stand, that it gives light to all who are in the house. Even so, let your light shine before others, that they may see your good works, and glorify your Father in heaven.

Salt is good for many things unless it becomes tainted with impurities; then it is good for nothing. In the same way, light is only useful if it is in the open rather than hidden. Christians are often thought of as narrow-minded, bigoted, unloving and resistant to change. What would it look like to be salt and light in today's world?

Prayer: Convict me, Lord, when my life communicates all the wrong messages.

Fulfilling the Law[38]

"Don't think I came to destroy the law or the prophets. I didn't come to destroy, but to fulfill. Until heaven and earth pass away, not even the smallest letter of the law shall pass away until everything is accomplished. Whoever breaks one of the least of these commandments, and teaches others to do so, shall be called least in the kingdom of God; whoever obeys and teaches them shall be called great. Unless your righteousness exceeds that of the scribes and Pharisees, there is no way you will enter into the kingdom of God.

Jesus managed to fulfill the law without being puritanical about it. We can do the same by understanding that the essence of the law is love, not rules. Are you a rule follower? Do you become resentful when you follow the rules and receive no reward while others break the rules and receive no punishment?

Prayer: Help me understand, Lord, that following your law is its own reward.

Murder and Rage[39]

"You have heard it said, 'You shall not murder;' and 'Whoever murders will be in danger of judgment.' But I tell you, everyone who is angry without cause will be in danger of judgment; and whoever says, 'Idiot!' will be in danger of the court; and whoever curses another will be in danger of the fire of hell.

---

[37] Matthew 5:13-16; Mark 4:21; Luke 11:33
[38] Matthew 5:17-20
[39] Matthew 5:21-26; Luke 12:57-59

Almost anything can rupture a relationship. Too many people are determined to prove they are right no matter the cost. How often do you find yourself getting angry? How hard do you fight to prove you are right? How often do you say things in anger you later regret?

Prayer: Get me back on track, Lord, when my defensiveness makes me start attacking others.

"If you are offering your gift at the altar, and remember that someone has something against you, leave your gift there, and go be reconciled to that person; then come and offer your gift."

"Settle your financial disputes quickly, while you are with your adversary on the road, lest the prosecutor deliver you to the judge, and the judge deliver you to the officer, and you be cast into prison. You shall not get out of there until you have paid the last penny."

Acting with Integrity[40]

"You have heard it said, 'You shall not commit adultery;' but I tell you if you look lustfully at another, you have already committed adultery in your heart. If your right eye causes you to stumble, pluck it out and throw it away. It is better that part of you should perish, than for your whole body to be cast into hell. If your right hand causes you to stumble, cut it off; it is better to be maimed than to be cast into hell.

Being a rule follower tempts us to justify doing what we want by finding loopholes and technicalities. Being faithful means acting with integrity in all we do. Do you recognize in yourself the temptation to circumvent rules? Do you find it easier to make excuses than to admit guilt?

Prayer: Confront me, Lord, when I fail to live with honor and integrity.

"It was also said, 'Whoever shall put away his wife, must give her a certificate of divorce,' but I tell you that whoever divorces his wife, except for the cause of sexual immorality, makes her an adulterer; and whoever marries a divorced person commits adultery."

"Again you have heard it was said, 'You shall not make false vows, but shall perform to the Lord your vows,' but I tell you, don't swear at all: neither by heaven, for it is the throne of God; nor by the earth, for it is his footstool; nor by Jerusalem, for it is the city of the great King. Neither shall you swear by your head, for you can't make one hair white or black.

[40] Matthew 5:27-42

But let your 'Yes' be 'Yes' and your 'No' be 'No.' Whatever is more than this is of the evil one."

Outrageous Love[41]

"You have heard it said, 'An eye for an eye, and a tooth for a tooth.' But I tell you, don't resist anyone who is evil; if someone strikes you on your right cheek, turn the other also. If anyone sues you to take away your coat, give up your cloak also. Whoever compels you to go one mile, go a second one. Give to those who ask you, and don't turn away anyone who wants to borrow from you. If you lend to those from whom you hope to receive, what credit is that to you? Even sinners lend to sinners, to receive back even more. If you love those who love you, and do good to those who do good to you, what credit is that to you? Even sinners do the same. If you only greet your friends, what more do you do than others? Don't even tax collectors do the same?

There is nothing more outrageous than loving your enemy. Many explain away this teaching, arguing that Jesus never meant it to be taken literally. Jesus lived it, though, even to the point of asking God to forgive the people who nailed him to the cross. Do you have trouble with this command? What people do you find hardest to love?

Prayer: Help me understand, Lord, that even my enemies are not beyond the scope of your love.

"You have heard it said, 'You shall love your neighbor and hate your enemy.' But I tell you, love your enemies, bless those who curse you, do good to those who hate you, and pray for those who mistreat you and persecute you, that you may be children of your Father who is in heaven.

"Love your enemies, and do good; lend, expecting nothing back. Your reward will be great, and you will be children of the Most High; for he is kind toward the ungrateful and wicked. God makes his sun to rise on the evil and the good, and sends rain on the just and the unjust. Be merciful, even as your Father is merciful. Be whole and complete, just as your Father in heaven is whole and complete.

Humble Charity[42]

"Be careful you don't do your giving before others, to be seen by them, or you'll have no reward from your Father in heaven. When you

---

41 Matthew 5:43-48; Luke 6:27-36
42 Matthew 6:1-4

show compassion, don't sound a trumpet, as the hypocrites do in the synagogues and in the streets, that they may get glory from others. You can be sure they have received their reward. But when you do merciful deeds, don't let your left hand know what your right hand does, so that the good you do may be done quietly; your Father who sees everything will reward you openly."

Few people find it easy to be humble. Do you become upset when those you help fail to be sufficiently grateful? How important to you is it to be recognized for the good you do?

Prayer: Help me, Lord, do good for goodness sake and not for enhancing my status in the eyes of others.

Prayer and Fasting[43]

"When you pray, don't be like the hypocrites who love to stand and pray in the synagogues and on the street corners to be seen by people. They have received their reward. But when you pray, enter your inner room, and having shut your door, pray to your Father in secret; your Father, who sees in secret, will reward you openly. When praying, don't use mindless repetitions, as the Gentiles do; they think they will be heard for their many words. Don't be like them; your Father knows what you need even before you ask. Pray like this: 'Our Father in heaven, may your name be kept holy. Let your kingdom come, let your will be done, on earth as it is in heaven. Give us today our daily bread. Forgive us our sins, as we also forgive those who sin against us. Bring us not into temptation, but deliver us from the evil one. For yours is the kingdom, the power, and the glory forever. Amen. '

"If you forgive others their sins, your heavenly Father will also forgive you. But if you don't forgive others their sins, neither will your Father forgive yours.

Jesus warned against "vain repetition" in prayers, saying the same thing over and over. Do you find yourself praying that way? What could you do to make your conversations with God less repetitive?

Prayer: Forgive me, Lord, when my prayers to you sound like I'm just going through the motions.

"When you fast, don't be like the hypocrites with sad faces, disfigured to be admired by others; they have received their reward. When you fast, anoint your head, and wash your face; so that you are not

[43] Matthew 6:5-18; Luke 11:1-4

seen to be fasting; your Father, who sees everything, will reward you.

True Wealth[44]

"Don't seek treasures for yourselves on earth, where moth and rust consume, and where thieves break in and steal; seek treasures in heaven, where neither moth nor rust consume, and where thieves don't break in and steal. Where your treasure is, there your heart will be also.

"The lamp of the body is the eye. If your eye is sound, your whole body will be full of light, but if your eye is evil, your whole body will be full of darkness. If the light in you is darkness, how great is the darkness!

"Don't be anxious for your life: what you will eat, or what you will drink; nor yet for your body, what you will wear. Isn't life more than food, and the body more than clothes? See the birds of the sky: they don't sow, nor reap, nor gather into barns. Your heavenly Father feeds them. Aren't you of much more value than they are?

"Which of you, by being anxious, can add one moment to your life? Why are you anxious about clothes? Consider how lilies of the field grow: they don't toil, neither do they spin, yet even Solomon in all his glory was not dressed like one of them. If God so clothes the grass of the field, which is here today, and gone tomorrow, won't God clothe you even though your faith is small?

"Therefore don't be anxious, saying, 'What will we eat?', 'What will we drink?' or, 'What will we wear?' The Gentiles seek all these things; your heavenly Father knows what you need. Seek first God's kingdom, and his righteousness, and all these things will be given you as well. Don't be anxious about tomorrow; each day has enough problems of its own.

How much is enough? Wealth is not evil in its essence, but is seductive because it never delivers as much happiness as it promises. How do you react to reading what Jesus says about wealth? Do you compare yourself to billionaires or beggars when deciding if you are wealthy?

Prayer: Save me, Lord, from a life in which more is never enough.

Grace-Filled Living[45]

"Don't judge, and you won't be judged. By whatever standard you judge others, you will be judged yourself; whatever measure you use for

---

[44] Matthew 6:19-34; Luke 11:34-36; Luke 12:22-34

[45] Matthew 7:1-11; Luke 6:41-42

others will be used for you. Why do you see the speck of dust in another's eye, but don't consider the beam that is in your own? Or how will you tell someone, 'Let me remove the speck from your eye' when you have a beam in your own? You hypocrite! First remove the beam out of your own eye, and then you can see clearly to remove the speck out of another's eye.

Do you find it easier to see the faults of others than your own? Do you extend to others the grace (unconditional love) God extends to you?

Prayer: Open my eyes to see my faults, Lord, and open my heart to receive the good gifts that come through your grace.

"Don't give what is holy to dogs, nor throw your pearls before pigs, lest they fail to appreciate them and come after you instead.

"Ask, and it will be given you. Seek, and you will find. Knock, and it will be opened for you. For everyone who asks, receives. Whoever seeks, finds. To anyone who knocks, the door will be opened. Is there any among you, who, if your children ask for bread, will give them a stone? Or if they ask for a fish, will give them a serpent? If you then, being evil, know how to give good gifts to your children, how much more will your Father in heaven give good things to those who ask him!

The Path to Goodness[46]

"Enter in by the narrow gate; for wide is the gate and broad is the way that leads to destruction, and many are those who enter in by it. Narrow is the gate, and difficult is the way that leads to life! Few are those who find it.

Things are not always what they appear to be: popular paths may be dangerous; evil can be disguised as something harmless; fruit may look good, but taste bitter; the outwardly religious may not be inwardly transformed. How well do you discern the right path and the right friends?

Prayer: Put me on the right path, Lord, that I might not lose my way.

"Beware of false prophets, who come to you in sheep's clothing, but inwardly are ravenous wolves. By their fruits you will know them. Do you gather grapes from thorns, or figs from thistles? Every good tree produces good fruit, but the sick tree produces bad fruit. A good tree can't produce bad fruit, neither can a sick tree produce good fruit.

Every tree that doesn't grow good fruit is cut down, and thrown into the fire.

---

[46] Matthew 7:13-23

By their fruits you will know them. Not everyone who says to me, 'Lord, Lord,' will enter into the kingdom of God; but those who do the will of my Father who is in heaven. Many will tell me in that day, 'Lord, Lord, didn't we prophesy in your name, cast out evil spirits in your name, and do many mighty works in your name?' Then I will tell them, 'I never knew you. Depart from me, you who work evil.'

A Solid Foundation[47]

"Everyone who comes to me and hears these words of mine, and then does them, is like a wise person, who built a house on rock. The rain came down, the floods came, and the winds blew, and beat on that house; it didn't fall, because it was founded on rock. Everyone who hears these words of mine, and doesn't do them will be like a foolish person, who built a house on sand. The rain came down, the floods came, and the winds blew, and beat on that house and it fell—and great was its fall."

When Jesus had finished saying these things, the multitudes were astonished at his teaching, for he taught them with authority, and not like the scribes.

The key difference between lives built on solid rock or shifting sands is whether the builder puts into practice what Jesus has said. When you hear the words of Jesus, do you consider how to apply them in your life? Do you find it easier to learn about Jesus than to learn from him?

Prayer: Show me, Lord, how to do what you say and not end up being foolish.

---

[47] Matthew 7:24-29; Luke 6:46-49

Chapter 5: Miracles and Parables

Blessings and Woes[48]

Jesus stood on a level place, with a crowd of his disciples, and a great number of people from all Judea and Jerusalem, and the sea coast of Tyre and Sidon, who came to hear him and to be healed of their diseases; as well as those who were troubled by unclean spirits. The multitude sought to touch him, for power came from him and healed them all.

The kingdom of God as explained by Jesus is like an upside-down version of the world: those who are powerful and corrupt now will be humbled and those who are oppressed now will be lifted up. Such a message, not surprisingly, was wildly popular with some and hated by others. How do you react to this list of blessings and woes? Where do you fit in?

Prayer: Help me be excited, Lord, not for the world as it is, but for the world as you would have it be.

He lifted up his eyes to his disciples, and said,

"Blessed are you who are poor;
God's kingdom is yours.
But woe to you who are rich!
For you have received your consolation.
Blessed are you who hunger now,
for you will be filled.
But woe to you, you who are full now,
for you will be hungry.
Blessed are you who weep now,
for you will laugh.
But woe to you who laugh now,
for you will mourn and weep.

"Blessed are you when, for the Son of Man's sake, people hate you, and exclude you, and mock you, and throw out your name as evil. Rejoice in that day, and leap for joy: your reward is great in heaven, for their

[48] Matthew 5:11-12; Luke 6:17-26

fathers did the same thing to the prophets. But woe to you when everyone speaks well of you, for their fathers did the same thing to the false prophets."

The Golden Rule[49]

"Whatever you would like others to do to you, do also to them; for this is the law and the prophets."

"Don't judge, and you won't be judged. Don't condemn, and you won't be condemned. Set others free, and you will be set free."

"Give, and it will be given to you: good measure, pressed down, shaken together, and running over. The measure you give will be given back to you."

He spoke a parable to them. "Can the blind guide the blind? Won't they both fall into a pit? Disciples are not above their teacher, but when fully trained will be like their teacher."

There is certainly nothing difficult to understand about the Golden Rule: treat others as you would like to be treated. Putting it into practice, however, is full of challenges. When do you find the Golden Rule most difficult to follow? Has someone in your life been a model for how this is done? Have you ever expressed appreciation to that person?

Prayer: Humble me, Lord, whenever I fail to treat others in the way I would like to be treated.

The Centurion's Servant[50]

After Jesus had finished speaking, he went to Capernaum, where a centurion's servant, who was dear to him, was sick and at the point of death. When the centurion heard about Jesus, he sent elders of the Jews to him, asking him to come and save his servant. When the elders came to Jesus, they pleaded with him, saying, "This man is worthy of your help; he loves our nation, and built our synagogue for us."

Jesus went with them. When he was not far from the house, the centurion

---

It is remarkable that leaders of a synagogue would speak highly of a Roman officer, given the hatred Jews felt toward their oppressors, but this was an unusual man. He could have heartlessly replaced his servant with another; instead, he wanted the servant to be healed. Have your preconceived ideas toward people of a different race, religion, ethnic group, political party or sexual orientation been at odds with someone you've come to know? How has that affected you?

Prayer: Bring into my life, Lord, those who will challenge my prejudices.

---

[49] Matthew 7:12; Luke 6:37-40

[50] Matthew 8:5-13; Luke 7:1-10; John 4:46-54

sent friends, saying, "Master, don't trouble yourself, for I am not worthy for you to come under my roof. I'm not even worthy to come to you; say the word, and my servant will be healed. For I also am a man with authority over soldiers. I tell this one, 'Go!' and he goes; and to another, 'Come!' and he comes; and to my servant, 'Do this,' and he does it."

When Jesus was told this, he marveled at what he heard, and turned and said to the multitude who followed him, "I tell you, I have not found such great faith anywhere in Israel." Those who were sent returned to the house and found the servant was now well.

The Widow's Son[51]

Soon afterwards, he went to a city called Nain. Many of his disciples, along with a large crowd, went with him. When he came near to the gate of the city, he met a funeral procession of people mourning for the only son of a widow. When Jesus saw her, he had compassion for her, and said, "Don't cry." He came near and touched the coffin, and the bearers stood still. He said, "Young man, I tell you, arise!" The boy sat up, and began to speak. Jesus gave him back to his mother.

All were amazed and praised God, saying, "A great prophet has arisen among us!" and, "God has visited his people!" This report went out concerning him in all Judea, and throughout the surrounding region.

As will be seen later with the raising of Lazarus, this was not a resurrection involving a new body, but bringing life back to an existing body. Do you know someone who has had a near death experience? How do you react when you hear about something defying medical explanation? Do you assume science will eventually figure out what happened?

Prayer: Keep me open, Lord, to the mysteries of life and death.

Stilling the Storm[52]

That evening, Jesus said to his disciples, "Let's go over to the other side." Leaving the multitude, they took him with them in the boat. Other small boats were also with them. A strong storm arose, waves were coming into the boat, and the boat began filling up. Jesus was in the stern, asleep on a cushion, when they woke him, saying, "Teacher, don't you care that we are dying?"

---

[51] Luke 7:11-17

[52] Matthew 8:23-27; Mark 4:35-41; Luke 8:22-25

He awoke, and rebuked the wind, and said to the sea, "Peace! Be still!" The wind ceased, and there was a great calm. He said to them, "Why are you so afraid? How is it that you have no faith?"

They were greatly afraid, and said to one another, "Who is this, that even the wind and the sea obey him?"

The disciples were afraid here of two things: the power of a storm which could kill them, and the power of Jesus which could calm the storm and save them. What threats to life do you fear most? Do people today still fear God? Should they?

Prayer: Save me, Lord, from presuming on your love or fearing your anger.

The Gadarene Deliverance[53]

They arrived at the country of the Gadarenes, which is opposite Galilee. When Jesus stepped ashore, a man who had been troubled by evil spirits for a long time met him. He wore no clothes, and didn't live in a house, but in the tombs.

When the man saw Jesus, he cried out and fell down before him, saying with a loud voice, "What do I have to do with you, Jesus, Son of the Most High God? I beg you, don't torment me!" For Jesus was commanding the unclean spirit to come out of the man. The unclean spirit had often seized the man who, when kept under guard and bound with chains and fetters, would break the bands apart and be driven by the evil spirit into the desert.

Jesus asked him, "What is your name?"

He said, "Legion," for many evil spirits had entered into him. They begged him that he would not command them to go into the abyss, but be allowed to enter into a herd of many pigs feeding on the mountain. He allowed them, and the evil spirits came out of the man and entered into the pigs. The herd rushed down the steep bank into the lake, and were drowned. When those who fed them saw what had happened, they fled, and told it in the city and in the country.

People went out to see what had happened. They came to Jesus, and found the man from whom the evil spirits had

Here was a naked wild man, once a danger to himself and others, now healed of the evil within him, and sitting at the feet of Jesus, clothed and in his right mind. Does this story connect with the epidemic of violence we see in our world? Is there hope that those caught up in today's crazed culture of violence could ever be delivered?

Prayer: Let your grace and peace, Lord, flow down on our crazed world.

[53] Matthew 8:28-34; Mark 5:1-20; Luke 8:26-39

gone sitting at Jesus' feet, clothed and in his right mind; they were amazed. Those who saw it told how the man possessed by evil spirits had been healed. All the people of the surrounding country of the Gadarenes asked him to depart from them, for they were very much afraid. Jesus entered into the boat; the man who had been healed begged to go with him, but Jesus sent him away, saying, "Return to your house, and declare what great things God has done for you." The man went his way, proclaiming throughout the whole city what had happened.

A Girl and a Woman[54]

When Jesus had crossed over in the boat to the other side, a great crowd came to him by the sea. Jairus, one of the rulers of the synagogue, came and fell at his feet, saying, "My daughter is at the point of death. Please come and lay your hands on her, that she may be healed, and live."

Jesus went with him, and a large crowd followed, pressing against him on all sides. In the crowd was a woman who had experienced a menstrual bleed for twelve years, suffering from many doctors' treatments, and spending all she had while getting worse, not better. Having heard about Jesus, she came up behind him in the crowd, and touched the fringe of his clothes, thinking, "If I just touch his clothes, I'll be made well." Immediately the flow of her blood was dried up, and she felt in her body that she was healed of her affliction.

Jesus, perceiving that power had gone out from him, turned around in the crowd, and asked, "Who touched me?"

His disciples said to him, "You see the crowd pressing against you, and you say, 'Who touched me?'"

But Jesus said, "Someone touched me, because power has gone out of me." He looked around to see who had done this. The woman, in fear and trembling at what she had done, came and fell down before him, and told him everything.

He said to her, "Daughter, your faith has made you well. Go in peace, and be cured of your disease."

While he was still speaking, people from the synagogue ruler's house came saying, "Your daughter is dead. Why bother the Teacher anymore?"

When Jesus heard the message, he said to Jairus, "Don't be afraid; only believe." He allowed no one to follow him, except Peter, James, and

---

[54] Matthew 9:18-26; Mark 5:21-43; Luke 8:40-56

John. Coming to the house, he saw an uproar with weeping and great wailing. When he had entered the house, he said to them, "Why do you make an uproar and weep? The child is not dead, but is asleep."

They ridiculed him. But having sent them outside, he took the child's father, mother, and those who were with them, and went in where the child was lying. Taking her by the hand, he said, "Talitha cumi!" which means, "Girl, I tell you, get up!" Immediately the girl, who was twelve years old, rose up and walked. They were amazed. He told them no one should know this, and said something should be given her to eat.

Jesus had a reputation as a healer, and yet there was often opposition to him. In this story, some ridiculed him when he said Jairus' daughter was not dead, but asleep. Do you think of yourself as a negative person? How would others describe you in this regard? What creates a negative attitude in people?

Prayer: Stop me, Lord, whenever I am tempted to make fun of others to cover up the pain in my own life.

Unforgivable Sin[55]

As Jesus went on from there, two blind men followed him, calling out, "Have mercy on us, Son of David!"

When he stopped and entered a house, the blind men came to him, and he asked them, "Do you believe I am able to do this?"

"Yes, Lord," they replied.

Then he touched their eyes and said, "According to your faith, let it be done to you." After their sight was restored, Jesus warned them sternly, "See that no one knows about this." But they went out and spread the news about him all over that region.

Someone possessed by an evil spirit, blind and mute, was brought to Jesus and healed so that he could speak and see. The multitudes were amazed, and said, "Can this be the son of David?" But when the Pharisees heard it, they said, "This man does not cast out evil spirits, except by Beelzebul, the prince of evil spirits."

Knowing their thoughts, Jesus said to them, "Every kingdom divided against itself is brought to desolation, and every city or house divided against itself will not stand. If Satan casts out Satan, he is divided against himself. How then will his kingdom stand? If I cast out evil spirits by Beelzebul, by whom do your children cast them out? Therefore, they will

[55] Matthew 9:27-34; 12:22-37; Mark 3:22-30; Luke 6:43-45; 11:14-23

be your judges. But if I by the Spirit of God cast out evil spirits, then God's kingdom has come upon you. How can one enter into the house of the strong man, and plunder his goods, unless he first binds the strong man? Then he will plunder his house. "He who is not with me is against me, and he who doesn't gather with me, scatters.

The language of "a kingdom divided" was used by Abraham Lincoln to warn America on the eve of the Civil War. What examples do you see of division in church and society today? Are there groups today who are convinced their opponents are "of the devil?" How can those who can't tell the difference between God and Satan be forgiven?

Prayer: Slow me down, Lord, when I too quickly ascribe evil intentions to those who think differently than I do.

Every sin and blasphemy will be forgiven, but blasphemy against the Spirit will not be forgiven. Whoever speaks a word against the Son of Man will be forgiven, but whoever speaks against the Holy Spirit will not be forgiven, neither in this age, nor in the age to come.

"Either make the tree good, and its fruit good, or make the tree corrupt, and its fruit corrupt; for the tree is known by its fruit. You offspring of vipers, how can you, being evil, speak good things? For out of the abundance of the heart, the mouth speaks. The good man out of his good treasure brings out good things, and the evil man out of his evil treasure brings out evil things. People will give account in the Day of Judgment for every idle word they speak. By your words you will be justified, and by your words you will be condemned."

Laborers for the Harvest[56]

Jesus went about the cities and the villages, teaching in their synagogues, preaching the good news of the kingdom, and healing every disease and sickness among the people. When he saw the crowds, he was moved with compassion, because they were harassed and helpless, like sheep without a shepherd. He said to his disciples, "The harvest is plentiful, but the laborers are few. Ask the Lord of the harvest to send out more workers."

He called to himself his twelve disciples, and gave them authority over unclean spirits, to cast them out, and to heal every disease and sickness. He told them, "Don't go among the Gentiles or enter into any city of the Samaritans, but go to the lost sheep of the house of Israel. As

[56] Matthew 9:35-10:4; Mark 6:34

you go, proclaim, 'The kingdom of God is at hand!' Heal the sick, cleanse the lepers, and cast out evil spirits. Give freely because you received freely. Don't take any gold, silver, or brass in your money belts. Take no bag for your journey, neither two coats, nor shoes, nor staff, for the laborer is worthy to be paid. In whatever city or village you enter, find out who is worthy and stay with them. As you enter a home, greet it. If the household is worthy, let your peace come on it, but if it isn't worthy, let your peace return to you. Whoever doesn't receive you or hear your words, as you go out of that house or city, shake off the dust from your feet. I tell you, it will be more tolerable for the land of Sodom and Gomorrah in the Day of Judgment than for that city.

We live in an age in which fewer and fewer are interested in church and yet there is no shortage of people who could be described as "harassed and helpless, like sheep without a shepherd." How many of your friends and family think of themselves as living the good life? How many could be described as living lives of quiet desperation? Do you feel any sense of being called to bring them hope?

Prayer: Send forth workers, Lord, and make it clear if I'm to be one of them.

The Challenge of Discipleship[57]

"I send you out as sheep among wolves. Therefore be wise as serpents, and harmless as doves. Beware of people: for they will deliver you up to councils, and in their synagogues they will scourge you. You will even be brought before governors and kings for my sake, for a testimony to them and to the nations; the good news must be preached to all nations. When they deliver you up, don't be anxious about what to say, for it will be given you; it won't be you who speaks, but the Spirit of your Father who speaks in you.

"Do you think I have come to bring peace on earth? Not peace, but rather division. For from now on, there will be five in one house divided, three against two. They will be divided, parents against children and children against parents."

"Those who come to me, and don't disregard father, mother, wife, children, brothers, and sisters, yes, and their own lives also, can't be my disciples. Those who don't bear their own crosses, and come after me, can't be my disciples.

"Brother will deliver up brother to death, and the father his child.

[57] Matthew 10:17-41; Mark 13:9-13; Luke 12:1-12; 12:49-53

Jesus was loved by some and hated by others; he made it clear those who followed him should not expect anything less. How important is it to you to be respected by others? Are you willing to stand for what you believe is right even if your perspective upsets others?

Prayer: Keep me strong, Lord, when following you upsets my family and friends.

Children will rise up against parents, and cause them to be put to death. You will be hated by all for my name's sake, but those who endure to the end will be saved. When they persecute you in one city, flee to the next; you will not have gone through the cities of Israel, before the Son of Man comes.

"Disciples are not above their teacher, nor servants above their lord. It is enough for the disciple to be like the teacher, and the servant like the lord. If they have called the master of the house Beelzebul, how much more his disciples!

There is nothing covered up that will not be revealed, nothing hidden that will not be known. Whatever you have said in the darkness will be heard in the light. What you have whispered indoors will be proclaimed from the housetops.

"Everyone who confesses me before others, the Son of Man will also confess before the angels of God; but those who deny me in the presence of others will be denied in the presence of the angels.

"Don't be afraid of those who kill the body, and after that can do no more. This is whom you should fear: the one who after you are dead has power to cast into hell. Yes, fear him.

"Aren't five sparrows sold for two pennies? Yet not one of them is forgotten by God. The very hairs of your head are all numbered. Don't be afraid: you are of more value than many sparrows.

The answer to John's question seems obvious, but things are always clearer in hindsight. Jesus wasn't what John had expected, and that raised questions for him. What preconceived ideas about Jesus do you bring to this study? Are you willing to let the actual story of Jesus change your thoughts about who he is and your relationship with him?

Prayer: Break through my preconceived ideas, Lord, and let me see you as you are even when it is different than what I've always thought.

Are You the One?[58]

When Jesus had finished directing his twelve disciples, he departed from there to teach and preach. When John heard in prison what Jesus was doing, he called two of his disciples and sent them to him. When the men had come to Jesus,

[58] Matthew 11:1-6; Luke 7:18-23

they said, "John the Baptizer has sent us to you, saying, 'Are you the one who comes, or should we look for another?'"

That day Jesus cured many of diseases and plagues and evil spirits, and gave sight to many who were blind. He said to the messengers, "Go and tell John what you have seen and heard: the blind receive their sight, the lame walk, the lepers are cleansed, the deaf hear, the dead are raised up, and the poor have good news preached to them. Blessed is he who finds no occasion for stumbling in me."

Comments on John the Baptizer[59]

When John's messengers had departed, he began to tell the crowds about John, "What did you go out into the wilderness to see? A reed shaken by the wind? A man in fine clothing? No, those who are fashionably dressed, and live elegantly, are in kings' courts. What did you go out to see? A prophet? Yes, and much more than a prophet. This is the one of whom it is written,

'Behold, I send my messenger before your face,
who will prepare your way before you.'

"Among those who are born of women there is not a greater prophet than John the Baptizer, yet he who is least in God's kingdom is greater than he."

When all the people and the tax collectors heard this, they declared God to be righteous, having been baptized with John's baptism. But the Pharisees and the lawyers rejected the counsel of God, not being baptized by him themselves.

"To what then shall I compare the people of this generation? They are like children who sit in the marketplace, and call to one another, saying, 'We piped to you, and you didn't dance. We mourned, and you didn't weep.' For John the Baptizer came neither eating bread nor drinking wine, and you say, 'He has an evil spirit.' The Son of Man has come eating and drinking, and you say, 'Behold, a gluttonous man, and a drunkard, a

John and Jesus were strongly connected to each other even though they were very different. John was criticized by some for being too austere; Jesus for not being austere enough. How badly do you want people to hold you in high regard? What does it cost you to try to please everybody?

Prayer: Set me free, Lord, from thinking my happiness depends on everyone liking me.

59 Matthew 11:7-19; Luke 7:24-35

friend of tax collectors and sinners!' Wisdom is justified by all her children."

Challenge and Invitation[60]

Jesus began to denounce the cities in which most of his mighty works had been done, because they didn't repent. "Woe to you, Chorazin! Woe to you, Bethsaida! For if the mighty works had been done in Tyre and Sidon which were done in you, they would have repented long ago in sackcloth and ashes. But I tell you, it will be more tolerable for Tyre and Sidon on the Day of Judgment than for you. You, Capernaum, who are exalted to heaven, you will go down to Hades. For if the mighty works had been done in Sodom which were done in you, it would have remained until today. But I tell you that it will be more tolerable for the land of Sodom, on the Day of Judgment, than for you."

At that time, Jesus prayed, "I thank you, Father, Lord of heaven and earth, that you hid these things from the wise and learned, and revealed them to children. Yes, Father, for so it was well-pleasing in your sight.

Jesus said, "All things have been delivered to me by my Father. No one knows the Son, except the Father; neither does anyone know the Father, except the Son, and those to whom the Son desires to reveal him.

"Come to me, all you who labor and are heavily burdened, and I will give you rest. Take my yoke upon you, and learn from me; I am gentle and humble in heart; and you will find rest for your souls. My yoke is easy, and my burden is light."

Jesus spoke harsh words to those in positions of power and privilege who refused to respond in faith even when Jesus did miracles in their midst. His message to those in distress, however, was a tender and gentle invitation to come and find rest. What parallels can you think of today? Would you be more comfortable issuing a challenge to those in power or offering hope to those in distress?

Prayer: Show me the right message, Lord, for those who find themselves in very different situations.

A Grateful Woman[61]

One of the Pharisees invited Jesus to eat with him. He entered the Pharisee's house and sat at the table. A woman in the city who was a sinner, when she knew he was reclining in the Pharisee's house, brought

[60] Matthew 11:20-30; Luke 10:13-16; 21-24
[61] Luke 7:36-50

an alabaster jar of ointment. Standing behind him and weeping, she began to wet his feet with her tears and wipe them with her long hair; she kissed and anointed his feet with the ointment. When the Pharisee who had invited him saw it, he thought to himself, "If this man were a prophet, he would have known how sinful this woman is who touches him."

Jesus said to him, "Simon, I have something to tell you."

He said, "Teacher, say on."

"A certain lender had two debtors. One owed him five hundred day's wages, and the other fifty. When they couldn't pay, he forgave them both. Which of them will love him most?"

Simon answered, "I suppose the one he forgave the most."

He said to him, "You have judged correctly." Turning to the woman, he said to Simon, "Do you see this woman? I entered your house, and you gave me no water for my feet, but she has wet my feet with her tears, and wiped them with her hair. You gave me no kiss, but since the time I came in, she has not stopped kissing my feet. You didn't anoint my head with oil, but she has anointed my feet with ointment. Therefore I tell you, her sins, which are many, are forgiven, for she loved much. But to whom little is forgiven, the same loves little." He said to her, "Your sins are forgiven."

The only thing we know about this woman is that the Pharisee saw her as a prostitute or harlot, while Jesus saw her as something entirely different. The way Jesus saw her had a profound impact on her life. Was there a moment when you knew God loved you in spite of everything you'd done and everything that had been done to you? How did that moment change you?

Prayer: Thank you, Lord, for seeing me differently than anyone else sees me.

Those who sat at the table with him began to say to themselves, "Who is this who even forgives sins?"

He said to the woman, "Your faith has saved you. Go in peace."

The Sign of Jonah[62]

Jesus went about through cities and villages, preaching and bringing the good news of God's kingdom. With him were the twelve, and women who had been healed of evil spirits and infirmities: Mary Magdalene, from whom seven evil spirits had gone out; Joanna, the wife of Herod's

---

62 Matthew 12:38-45; 16:1-4; Mark 8:11-12; Luke 8:1-3; 11:16, 24-26. 29-32

steward; Susanna; and many others who served him from their possessions.

Certain of the scribes and Pharisees came to Jesus and said, "Teacher, we want to see a sign from you."

But he answered them, "An evil and adulterous generation seeks after a sign, but no sign will be given it except the sign of Jonah the prophet. For as Jonah was three days and nights in the belly of the whale, so will the Son of Man be three days and nights in the heart of the earth. The men of Nineveh will stand up in the judgment with this generation, and will condemn it, because they repented at the preaching of Jonah, and someone greater than Jonah is here. The queen of the south will rise up in the judgment with this generation, and will condemn it, for she came from the ends of the earth to hear the wisdom of Solomon, and someone greater than Solomon is here.

When Jesus was tempted by the devil in the wilderness to jump from the pinnacle of the temple to see if God would save him, he said he would not ask for such a sign from God. Those who came to Jesus asking for a sign had succumbed to the temptation. Have you seen miraculous signs of God's presence in the world? Do you think it would be easier for you to follow God if you witnessed an undeniable miracle?

Prayer: Help me recognize the signs of your presence all around me, Lord, rather than asking for more.

When an unclean spirit has gone out of a man, he passes through waterless places, seeking rest, and doesn't find it. Then he says, 'I will return into my house from which I came out,' and when he has come back, he finds it empty, swept, and put in order. Then he goes, and takes with himself seven other spirits more evil than he is, and they enter in and dwell there. The last state of that man becomes worse than the first. Even so will it be also to this evil generation."

Forever Family[63]

While he was yet speaking to the crowds, his mother and his brothers stood outside. One said to him, "Your mother and your brothers stand outside, seeking to speak to you."

Jesus is not disrespecting his family in this story as much as he is honoring his followers, those who listen to what he says and put it into practice. What does it mean to you to be counted among the family of Jesus through sharing his vision and values? Do you feel a sense of connection and intimacy with Jesus and with others who follow him?

Prayer: Thank you, Lord, for inviting me to be part of your family.

[63] Matthew 12:46-50; Mark 3:31-35

But he answered, "Who is my mother? Who are my brothers?" He stretched out his hand towards his disciples, and said, "Behold, my mother and my brothers! For whoever does the will of my Father who is in heaven, is my brother, and sister, and mother."

Readiness for the Kingdom[64]

Then Jesus told this parable: "A farmer went out to sow, and as he sowed, some seed fell by the road, and the birds came and devoured it. Others fell on the rocky ground, where it had little soil, and immediately it sprang up, because it had no depth of soil. When the sun had risen, it was scorched; and because it had no root, it withered away. Others fell among the thorns, and the thorns grew up, and choked it, and it yielded no fruit. Others fell into the good ground, and yielded fruit, growing and increasing. Some produced thirty times, some sixty times, and some one hundred times as much." He said, "Whoever has ears to hear, should listen."

The disciples came, and said to him, "Why do you speak in parables?"

He answered them, "To you it is given to know the mysteries of the kingdom of God, but it is not given to them. For those who have will be given more, and will have an abundance, but those who don't have, what little they have will be taken away. I speak to them in parables, because though they see, they don't see, and though they hear, they don't hear; neither do they understand. In them the prophecy of Isaiah is fulfilled, which says,

'By hearing you will hear,
  and will in no way understand;
Seeing you will see,
  and will in no way perceive:
for this people's heart has grown callous,
  their ears are dull of hearing,
  they have closed their eyes;
or else perhaps they might perceive with their eyes,
  hear with their ears,
  understand with their heart,
and would turn again;
  and I would heal them.'

---

64 Matthew 13:1-23; Mark 4:1-20; Luke 8:4-21

"But blessed are your eyes, for they see; and your ears, for they hear. Many prophets and righteous believers desired to see the things you see, and didn't see them, and to hear the things you hear, and didn't hear them.

"Don't you understand this parable? How will you understand any of the parables? The farmer sows the word. The ones by the road are the ones where the word is sown, and when they have heard, immediately Satan comes, and takes away the word which has been sown in them. So it is with the word sown on the rocky places: people receive it with joy, but have no root in themselves, and are short-lived; when oppression or persecution comes, they stumble. Others are those sown among the thorns; they hear the word, but the cares of this world, the deceitfulness of riches, and other desires choke the word, and it becomes unfruitful. Those sown on the good ground hear the word, accept it, and bear fruit, some thirty times, some sixty times, and some one hundred times."

The different kinds of soil may not be different kinds of people, as much as people at different stages in their lives. Have there been times in your life when you could identify with each of the four types? Can you think of people you know who fit in each of them now?

Prayer: Help me recognize, Lord, when people are at a point in their life where they are ready to hear and understand.

Speaking in Parables[65]

He said to them, "Is the lamp brought to be put under a basket or under a bed? Isn't it put on a stand? There is nothing hidden, that shouldn't be made known; neither was anything secret, that shouldn't come to light. Whoever has ears to hear, should listen."

"God's kingdom is as if you cast seed on the ground, and days go by, and the seed springs up and grows, but you don't know how. The earth bears fruit: first the blade, then the ear, then the full grain on the ear. When the fruit is ripe, you put in the sickle, because the harvest has come."

He told them another parable: "The kingdom of God is like a man who sowed good seed in his field, but at night, his enemy came and sowed weeds among the wheat, and went away. When the blade sprang up and produced grain, the weeds appeared also. The servants came and

[65] Matthew 13:24-35; Mark 4:22-34; Luke 8:9-19; 13:20-21

said to the farmer, 'Didn't you sow good seed in your field? Where did these weeds come from?'

"He said to them, 'An enemy has done this.'

"The servants asked him, 'Do you want us to go and gather them up?'

"But he said, 'No, because gathering up the weeds could harm the wheat. Let both grow together until the harvest, and in the harvest I will tell the reapers, "First, gather up the weeds, and bind them in bundles to burn them; but gather the wheat into my barn."'"

The nature of God's kingdom is hard for us to understand: we're not sure how it's growing, we don't always like the way it's growing, but ultimately we're amazed at how much it has grown! How do you rate your own grasp of God's kingdom? Do you see it coming in the world around you?

Prayer: Give me ears to hear, Lord, and a heart to understand the wonders of your kingdom.

He said, "How can we explain God's kingdom? Or with what parable can we illustrate it? It's like a grain of mustard seed, which is the smallest of seeds when it is sown in the earth, yet when it grows up, becomes greater than all the herbs, and puts out branches, so that birds of the sky can lodge under its shadow."

Again he said, "To what shall I compare God's kingdom? It is like yeast, which a woman took and hid in three measures of flour, until it was all leavened."

With many such parables he spoke to the crowds, as they were able to hear it. He rarely spoke to them except in parables; privately, he explained everything to his disciples, to fulfill what was spoken through the prophet:

"I will open my mouth in parables;
I will utter things hidden from the foundation of the world."

More Parables and Explanations[66]

Then Jesus sent the crowds away, and went into the house. His disciples came to him, saying, "Explain to us the parable of the weeds of the field."

He answered them, "He who sows the good seed is the Son of Man; the field is the world; the good seed are the children of the kingdom; the weeds are the children of the evil one. The enemy who sowed them is the devil. The harvest is the end of the age, and the reapers are angels. As the

[66] Matthew 13:36-52

weeds are gathered up and burned, so will it be at the end of this age. The Son of Man will send out his angels, and they will gather out of his kingdom all things that cause stumbling, and those who do iniquity, and will cast them into the furnace of fire. There will be weeping and gnashing of teeth. Then the righteous will shine like the sun in the kingdom of their Father. Whoever has ears to hear, should listen.

"Again, the kingdom of God is like a treasure hidden in the field, which a man found, and hid. In his joy, he goes and sells all that he has, and buys that field.

"Again, the kingdom of God is like a merchant seeking fine pearls, who having found one pearl of great price, sells everything to buy it.

"Again, the kingdom of God is like a dragnet cast into the sea, gathering fish of every kind. When the boat is filled, they draw up on the beach, sit down, gather the good into containers, and throw the bad away. So will it be at the end of the world. The angels will come and separate the wicked from the righteous, and cast them into the furnace of fire where there will be weeping and gnashing of teeth." Jesus said to them, "Have you understood all these things?"

The idea of hellfire is far more prevalent in the minds of many Christians than in the teachings of Jesus. The parables here speak of weeds being burned up and "bad fish" being thrown away; both speak of judgment, but neither speaks of eternal torment. What have you been taught about hell? Do you think fear of eternal torment brings anyone to God? Do you think lack of belief in judgment leads to lack of accountability?

Prayer: Keep me from the extremes, Lord, of needlessly fearing you or of presumptuously ignoring you.

They answered him, "Yes, Lord."

He said to them, "Every scribe who has been made a disciple in the kingdom of God is like a householder, who brings out treasures, new and old."

The Healing at the Pool[67]

After these things, there was a feast of the Jews, and Jesus went up to Jerusalem. Now in Jerusalem by the sheep gate, there is a pool, which is called in Hebrew, "Bethesda", having five porches. In these lay many who were sick, blind, lame, or paralyzed, waiting for the moving of the water; for an angel went down at certain times into the pool, and stirred

[67] John 5:1-18

up the water. Whoever stepped in first after the stirring of the water was healed of any disease.

A man was there, who had been sick for thirty-eight years. When Jesus saw him lying there, and knew that he had been sick for a long time, he asked him, "Do you want to be made well?"

The sick man answered him, "Sir, I have no one to put me into the pool when the water is stirred up, but while I'm coming, another steps down before me."

Jesus said to him, "Arise, take up your mat, and walk."

Immediately, the man was made well, and took up his mat and walked.

Now it was the Sabbath, and the Jews said to him, "It is not lawful for you to carry your mat on the Sabbath."

Here was a man with a great need who stayed near the healing waters of a pool he could never reach. The miracle for which he was hoping came in a way he never imagined. Has God ever stepped into your life at a moment of desperation when all seemed hopeless? If so, to how many people have you told your story?

Prayer: Give me boldness, Lord, to not hold back from telling others how you helped me at my time of greatest need.

He answered them, "The man who made me well said to me, 'Take up your mat, and walk.'"

Then they asked him, "Who is the man who said this to you?"

But the man who was healed didn't know who it was, for Jesus had withdrawn to avoid the crowd in that place.

Afterward Jesus found him in the temple, and said to him, "You are made well. Now sin no more, so that nothing worse happens to you."

The man went away, and told the Jews that it was Jesus who had made him well. Because this healing was on the Sabbath, the Jews persecuted Jesus, and sought to kill him. Jesus told them, "My Father is still working, so I am working too." Now the Jews sought all the more to kill him, because he not only broke the Sabbath, but also called God his own Father, making himself equal with God.

Doing What God Does[68]

Jesus told them, "The Son can do nothing of himself, but only what he sees the Father doing; whatever he does, the Son does likewise. The Father loves the Son, and shows him all things he himself does; he will even show him greater works than these that you may marvel. As the

[68] John 5:19-47

Father raises the dead and gives them life, even so the Son also gives life to whom he desires. For the Father judges no one, but he has given all judgment to the Son, that all may honor the Son, even as they honor the Father. Anyone who doesn't honor the Son doesn't honor the Father who sent him.

"Anyone who hears my word, and believes him who sent me, has eternal life, and doesn't come into judgment, but has passed out of death into life. The hour comes, and now is, when the dead will hear the Son of God's voice; those who hear will live. As the Father has life in himself, even so he gave to the Son also to have life in himself. He also gave him authority to execute judgment, because he is the Son of Man. Don't marvel at this, for the hour comes, when all in the tombs will hear his voice, and will come out; those who have done good, to the resurrection of life, and those who have done evil, to the resurrection of judgment. I can of myself do nothing. As I hear, I judge, and my judgment is right because I don't seek my own will, but the will of my Father who sent me.

"If I testify about myself, my witness is not valid. It is another who testifies about me. I know that the testimony which he gives about me is true. You have talked to John the Baptizer, and he has testified to the truth. The testimony I receive is not from anyone. I say these things that you may be saved. John was the burning and shining lamp, and you were willing to rejoice for a while in his light. But the testimony I give is greater than that of John; the works the Father gave me to do testify about me, that the Father has sent me. The Father himself, who sent me, has testified about me. You have neither heard his voice at any time, nor seen his form. You don't have his word living in you, because you don't believe him whom he sent.

Jesus made such outrageous claims about himself that it is hard not to conclude he had to be either seriously delusional or someone like no one else who ever lived. Nobody making such claims today could be taken seriously. How do you see Jesus? Do you understand him to be the person he claimed to be?

Prayer: Shock me out of complacency, Lord, when I begin to act as if your claims have no bearing on how I choose to live my life.

"You search the Scriptures, because you think in them you have eternal life; they testify about me, yet you will not come to me, that you may have life. I don't receive glory from men, and I know you don't have God's love in yourselves. I've come in my Father's name, and you don't receive me, yet you receive those who come in their own name. How can you believe when you receive glory from one another, and don't seek the glory that comes only from God?

"Don't think that I will accuse you to the Father. The one who accuses you is Moses, on whom you have set your hope. For if you believed Moses, you would believe me because he wrote about me. If you don't believe his writings, how will you believe my words?"

The Death of John the Baptizer[69]

Herod heard what was done by Jesus, and was perplexed because some said John the Baptizer had risen from the dead, others that Elijah had appeared, and still others that one of the prophets had come back. Herod said, "John I beheaded, but who is this, about whom I hear such things?" He wanted to see Jesus.

Herod had earlier arrested John, and bound him in prison for the sake of Herodias, his brother's wife, whom Herod had married. John said to Herod, "It is not lawful for you to live with your brother's wife." Herodias set herself against John and desired to kill him, but she couldn't because Herod feared John. Knowing John was a righteous and holy man, Herod kept him safe and liked to listen to him.

When Herod's birthday came, he had a feast for his nobles, high officers, and chief men of Galilee. When the daughter of Herodias came in and danced, she pleased Herod and those sitting with him. The king said to the young lady, "Ask me whatever you want, and I will give it to you." He swore to her, "Whatever you shall ask of me, I will give you, up to half of my kingdom."

Other than the Emperor, Herod was the supreme ruler in all of Judea. As so often is the case, however, his power didn't enable him to deny his wife or daughter what they wanted, nor was he able to "look weak" in front of his guests. Have you ever felt backed into a corner, forced to make what you knew was a bad choice in order to avoid being thought weak by others? How did it turn out?

Prayer: Give me the courage to do the right thing, Lord, rather than back down for fear of what others may think.

She went out, and said to her mother, "What shall I ask?"

She said, "The head of John the Baptizer."

She came in immediately with haste to the king, and asked, "I want you to give me right now the head of John the Baptizer on a platter."

---

[69] Matthew 14:1-12; Mark 6:12-29; Luke 3:19-20; 9:7-9

The king was exceedingly sorry, but for the sake of his oaths and his guests, didn't want to refuse her. The king sent a soldier of his guard, and told him to bring John's head. The soldier beheaded John in the prison, brought his head on a platter, and gave it to the young lady, who gave it to her mother.

When John's disciples heard this, they came and took up his corpse, and laid it in a tomb.

Feeding the 5,000[70]

After returning from their mission, the twelve came to Jesus and told him all they had done and everything they had taught. He said to them, "Come apart with me into a deserted place, and rest awhile." For there were many coming and going, and the disciples had no time even to eat.

Earlier Jesus had said he only could do what God does. The Hebrew Scriptures tell of God providing manna (bread-like food) in the wilderness, and other stories of God miraculously providing for his people. Has God ever met your needs in a situation that seemed hopeless? Have you ever told someone the story of what God did for you?

Prayer: When situations look hopeless, Lord, help me trust you to find a way through.

The disciples and Jesus went away in the boat to a deserted place. People saw them going, though, and ran there on foot from all the cities. They arrived before the disciples and came to Jesus. He saw a huge crowd, and had compassion on them, because they were like sheep without a shepherd; he began to teach them many things. When it was late in the day, his disciples said, "This place is deserted, and it is late. Send these people away, that they may go into the surrounding country and villages, and buy themselves bread, for they have nothing to eat."

But he answered them, "You give them something to eat."

They asked him, "Shall we go and buy two hundred day's wages worth of bread in order to give them something to eat?"

He said to them, "How many loaves do you have? Go see."

When they knew, they said, "Five, and two fish."

He told everyone to sit down in groups on the green grass. They sat down in ranks, by hundreds and by fifties. He took the five loaves and the two fish, and looking up to heaven, he blessed and broke the loaves, and he gave to his disciples to set before them, and he divided the two fish

[70] Matthew 14:13-21; Mark 6:30-44; Luke 9:10-17; John 6:1-15

among them all. After they all ate and were filled, they took up twelve baskets full of broken pieces of bread and fish. Those who ate the loaves were five thousand men.

Walking on Water[71]

Jesus told the disciples to get into the boat and go ahead of him to the other side. After he had sent the crowds away, he went up into the mountain by himself to pray. When evening came, he was there alone; the boat was now in the middle of the sea, distressed by the waves because the wind was fierce. Late in the night, Jesus came to them, walking on the sea. When the disciples saw him, they cried out in fear, "It's a ghost!" Jesus spoke to them, "Cheer up! It is I! Don't be afraid."

Peter answered him, "Lord, if it is you, let me to come to you on the waters."

He said, "Come!"

Peter stepped down from the boat, and walked on the waters toward Jesus. But when he saw that the wind was strong, he was afraid, and beginning to sink, cried out, "Lord, save me!"

In this story, Jesus is once again a non-anxious presence, unconcerned about wind and waves, walking on water toward the boat. Peter is able to walk on the water as well until his focus shifts from Jesus to the wind and waves. When the storms of life are raging, do you find it difficult to keep your focus and walk by faith? Can you think of an example in your own life when Jesus reached out and grabbed you when you were starting to sink?

Prayer: When the storms come, Lord, help me keep my focus and walk by faith.

Jesus stretched out his hand, took hold of him, and said, "You of little faith, why did you doubt?" When they got up into the boat, the wind ceased. Those who were in the boat came and worshiped him, saying, "You truly are the Son of God!"

The Bread of Life[72]

When they had crossed over, they landed at Gennesaret, and moored to the shore. People recognized Jesus, and came from the whole region, bringing those who were sick to where they heard he was. Wherever he went, into villages or cities or the countryside, they laid the sick in the marketplaces, and begged to touch just the fringe of his garment; many

[71] Matthew 14:22-33; Mark 6:45-52; John 6:16-21
[72] Matthew 14:34-46; Mark 6:53-56; John 6:22-40

touched him and were made well.

The crowd on the other side of the sea saw there was no other boat there except the one in which his disciples had embarked, and that Jesus hadn't entered with his disciples into the boat, but his disciples had gone away alone. When the multitude realized Jesus wasn't there, nor his disciples, they got into their boats, and came to Capernaum, seeking Jesus. When they found him on the other side of the sea, they asked him, "Rabbi, when did you come here?"

Jesus answered them, "You seek me, not because you saw signs, but because you ate of the loaves, and were filled. Don't work for the food which perishes, but for the food which remains to eternal life, which the Son of Man will give to you. For God the Father has authorized him."

They said to him, "What must we do to work the works of God?"

Jesus answered, "This is the work of God: believe in him whom he has sent."

They said to him, "What will you do for a sign, that we may see, and believe you? What work do you do? Our fathers ate the manna in the wilderness. As it is written, 'He gave them bread out of heaven to eat.'"

Jesus answered, "It wasn't Moses who gave you the bread out of heaven, but my Father gives you the true bread out of heaven. For the bread of God is that which comes down out of heaven, and gives life to the world."

They said to him, "Lord, always give us this bread."

People come to Jesus for different reasons. Some feel privileged to think they are being asked to do something for God; others have no interest in anything except what God can do for them. What first attracted you to Jesus? Fear of hell? Hope of heaven? The call of the kingdom?

Prayer: Keep me honest, Lord, when I am tempted to follow you for the wrong reasons.

Jesus said, "I am the bread of life. He who comes to me will not be hungry, and he who believes in me will never be thirsty. You have seen me, and yet you don't believe. All those whom the Father gives me will come to me. He who comes to me I will in no way reject. I have come down from heaven, not to do my own will, but the will of him who sent me. This is the will of my Father: that of all he has given me I should lose nothing; that everyone who sees the Son and believes in him should have eternal life; and that I will raise up all of them at the last day."

Murmurs of Unbelief[73]

The Jews murmured concerning him, because he said, "I am the bread which came down out of heaven." They said, "Isn't this Jesus, the son of Joseph, whose father and mother we know? How can he say, 'I have come down out of heaven?'"

Jesus answered them, "Don't murmur among yourselves. No one can come to me unless the Father who sent me draws him, and I will raise him up in the last day. It is written in the prophets, 'They will all be taught by God.' Therefore everyone who hears from the Father, and has learned, comes to me. Not that anyone has seen the Father, except the one who is from God. He has seen the Father. Whoever believes in me has eternal life.

I am the bread of life. Your fathers ate manna in the wilderness and died. This is the bread which comes down out of heaven that anyone may eat of it and not die. I am the living bread which came down out of heaven. Whoever eats of this bread will live forever. The bread I will give for the life of the world is my body."

The Jews said to one another, "How can this man give us his body to eat?"

Jesus said to them, "Unless you eat the flesh of the Son of Man and drink his blood, you don't have life in yourselves. Whoever eats my flesh and drinks my blood has eternal life, and will be raised up at the last day. My flesh is food, and my blood is drink. Those who eat my flesh and drink my blood live in me, and I in them. As the Father sent me, and I live because of the Father, so whoever feeds on me will also live because of me. This is the bread which came down out of heaven—not as our fathers ate manna, and died. Whoever eats this bread will live forever." He said these things in the synagogue, as he taught in Capernaum.

One of the biggest challenges in understanding the Bible is knowing what is meant to be literal and what is metaphorical. Early Christians were thought by some to be cannibals who worshipped by eating the body and blood of Jesus. Do you find the symbolism of bread and cup, body and blood, helpful and powerful or does it seem archaic and confusing? Would you have murmured with the others who first heard Jesus speak of such things?

Prayer: Let the bread and cup nourish me, Lord, even when I am unsure of all it means.

---

[73] John 6:41-66

Many of his disciples, when they heard this, said to one another, "This is a hard saying! Who can accept it?"

Jesus, knowing his disciples murmured at this, said to them, "Does this cause you to stumble? Then what if you would see the Son of Man ascending to where he was before? It is the spirit who gives life. The flesh profits nothing. The words that I speak to you are spirit, and are life. But there are some of you who don't believe." For Jesus knew from the beginning who didn't believe, and who would betray him. He said, "For this cause have I said to you that no one can come to me unless it has been made possible by my Father."

At this, many of his disciples went back, and walked no more with him.

Peter's Confession[74]

Jesus said to the twelve, "You don't also want to go away, do you?"

Simon Peter answered him, "Lord, to whom would we go? You have the words of eternal life. We have come to believe and know that you are the Christ, the Son of the living God."

Jesus answered them, "Didn't I choose you, the twelve, and one of you is a devil?" Now he spoke of Judas, the son of Simon Iscariot, for it was he who would betray him, being one of the twelve.

Now when Jesus came into Caesarea Philippi, he asked his disciples, saying, "Who do men say that I, the Son of Man, am?"

They said, "Some say John the Baptizer, some, Elijah, and others, Jeremiah, or one of the prophets."

He said to them, "But who do you say that I am?"

Simon Peter answered, "You are the Christ, the Son of the living God."

Jesus replied, "Blessed are you, Simon, for flesh and blood has not revealed this to you, but my Father in heaven. You are Peter, and on this

---

For centuries, Jewish prophets had told of the coming of a new kind of king who would lead a new kind of kingdom. This new king came to be referred to as the Promised One, the Messiah (Hebrew) or the Christ (Greek). The woman at the well had asked her neighbors, "Could this be the Messiah?" Peter went further and said, "You are the Messiah." How do you describe Jesus? A great man? A great teacher? The one whose coming fulfilled all the promises of God?

Prayer: Help me think clearly, Lord, about who you are – and who you are to me.

---

[74] Matthew 16:13-20; Mark 8:27-30; Luke 9:18-21; John 6:67-71

rock I will build my church, and the gates of Hades will not prevail against it. I will give you the keys of the kingdom of God, and whatever you bind on earth will be bound in heaven, and whatever you release on earth will be released in heaven." Then he commanded the disciples that they should tell no one that he was the Christ.

Take up Your Cross[75]

From that time, Jesus began to show his disciples that he must go to Jerusalem and suffer many things from the elders, chief priests, and scribes, and be killed, and the third day be raised up.

Peter took him aside, and began to rebuke him, saying, "Far be it from you, Lord! This will never happen to you."

But he turned, and said to Peter, "Get behind me, Satan! You are a stumbling block to me, for you are not setting your mind on the things of God, but on the things of the world."

He said to all, "You who desire to come after me, deny yourselves, take up your cross, and follow me. If you seek to save your life, you will lose it, but if you lose your life for my sake, you will save it. What does it profit you to gain the whole world, and lose your own self? Those who are ashamed of me and my words, of them will the Son of Man be ashamed when he comes in his glory, and the glory of the Father, and of the holy angels. There are some of those who stand here who will not taste death until they see God's kingdom."

Peter and the disciples could well imagine a series of triumphs in Jesus' future, but death on a cross was unimaginable. Many preachers today focus almost exclusively on prosperity. Do you think following Jesus should bring fame and fortune, or at least honor and respect? What would it look like for you to take up your cross and follow Jesus?

Prayer: Forgive me, Lord, for scripting my future in accordance with what I want rather than what you want and what your kingdom calls me to.

Voiding the Law[76]

Some Pharisees and scribes came to Jesus from Jerusalem. When they saw his disciples eating bread with defiled hands, they became critical. (Jews don't eat unless they wash their hands and forearms, according to the tradition of the elders. They bathe themselves before

[75] Matthew 16:21-28; Mark 8:31-9:1; Luke 9:22-27

[76] Matthew 15:1-20; Mark 7:1-23; Luke 11:37-54

eating when they come from the market, and hold to many other traditions: washings of cups, pitchers, bronze vessels, and couches.) The Pharisees and scribes asked him, "Why don't your disciples follow the tradition of the elders, but eat their bread with unwashed hands?"

He answered them, "Well did Isaiah prophesy of you hypocrites,

'This people honors me with their lips,
but their heart is far from me.
They worship me in vain,
teaching as doctrines the commandments of people.'

"You set aside the commandment of God, and hold tightly to the traditions—the washing of pitchers and cups, and you do many other such things." He said to them, "You reject the commandment of God to keep your tradition. Moses said, 'Honor your father and your mother;' and, 'Whoever speaks evil of father or mother should be put to death.' But you say, 'If a man tells his father or mother, "The help you might have received from me has been dedicated to God's use,"' then you no longer require him to do anything for his father or mother. You void the word of God by your tradition, and do many things like this."

He called to the crowd, and said, "Hear me, all of you, and understand. There is nothing from outside of someone, that going in can bring defilement; but the things which proceed out of the heart are what defiles a person. Those who have ears to hear, should listen!"

The disciples came, and said, "Do you know the Pharisees were offended when they heard this saying?"

But he answered, "Every plant which my heavenly Father didn't plant will be uprooted. Leave them alone. They are blind guides of the blind. If the blind lead the blind, both will fall into a pit."

When he had entered a house away from the crowd, his disciples asked about the parable. He said, "Don't you understand? Whatever goes into you from outside can't bring defilement because it doesn't go into your heart, but into your stomach and then out of the body? All foods are clean; it is what proceeds out of

---

Jesus had harsh words for those who spoke hypocritically of obeying the law while finding ways around it in their daily lives. Have you run into people who do this? Do you have favorite words of Jesus you follow closely and others you explain away or simply ignore?

Prayer: Convict me, Lord, when I begin twisting your teachings to fit my own preferences.

---

your heart that brings defilement: evil thoughts, adultery, sexual sin, murder, theft, covetings, wickedness, deceit, desires, an evil eye, blasphemy, pride, and foolishness. These evil things come from within, and defile you."

Woe to you Pharisees, who tithe mint and rue and every herb, but bypass justice and the love of God! You ought to have done the former without neglecting the other. Woe to you Pharisees, who love the best seats in the synagogues, and honored greetings in the marketplaces. Woe to you, scribes and Pharisees, hypocrites! You are like hidden graves people walk over without knowing."

One of the lawyers answered him, "Teacher, in saying this you insult us also."

He said, "Woe to you lawyers also! For you load men with burdens that are difficult to carry, and you won't even lift one finger to carry them. Woe to you who build monuments for the prophets your fathers killed, glorifying what they did. God said, 'I will send prophets and apostles; some of them they will kill and persecute. The blood of the prophets, shed from the foundation of the world, may be required of this generation: from the blood of Abel to the blood of Zachariah, who perished between the altar and the sanctuary.' Yes, it will be required of this generation. Woe to you lawyers, who took away the key of knowledge! You wouldn't enter in yourselves, and those who were entering, you hindered."

As he said these things to them, the scribes and the Pharisees began to be terribly angry, and to draw things out of him. They lay in wait for him, seeking to catch him in something he might say, in order to accuse him.

The Canaanite Woman[77]

Jesus left there, and went into the region of Tyre and Sidon. A Canaanite woman came from there, and cried, "Have mercy on me, Lord, son of David! My daughter is severely possessed by an evil spirit!"

But he answered her not a word.

His disciples came and begged him, "Send her away; for she cries after us."

---

[77] Matthew 15:21-28; Mark 7:24-30

He said, "I wasn't sent to anyone but the lost sheep of the house of Israel."

She came and worshiped him, saying, "Lord, help me."

But he answered, "It is not appropriate to take the children's bread and throw it to the dogs."

But she said, "Yes, Lord, but even the dogs eat the crumbs which fall from their masters' table."

Then Jesus answered her, "Woman, great is your faith! Let it be done as you want." And her daughter was healed from that hour.

The interaction between Jesus and this woman is hard for us to understand given the cultural gap between their time and our own. The disciples were annoyed and Jesus was perplexed until the situation was resolved through the woman's sincere faith and quick wit. Are you troubled by Jesus behaving in an uncharacteristic manner? Could Jesus be fully human and still in complete control of every situation?

Prayer: Help me realize, Lord, that not everything in your story is simple and easy to understand.

Healing a Deaf Mute[78]

Leaving the borders of Tyre and Sidon, Jesus came to the Sea of Galilee, through the middle of the region of Decapolis. People brought to him one who was deaf and had a speech impediment, and begged Jesus to lay his hand on him. Jesus took him aside from the multitude, privately, and put his fingers into his ears, and he spat, and touched his tongue. Looking up to heaven, he sighed, and said to him, "Ephphatha!" that is, "Be opened!" Immediately his ears were opened, and his tongue was released, and he spoke clearly. He commanded them to tell no one, but the more he commanded them, the more widely they proclaimed it. They were astonished beyond measure, saying, "He has done all things well. He makes even the deaf hear, and the mute speak!"

This man was given a new life and clear evidence life's afflictions aren't a punishment from God. How have you thought about the suffering in your life? What imperfections in your body would you most like to see changed?

Prayer: Thank you, Lord, for the wonders of the human body and the promise of a new body in the resurrection.

Feeding the 4,000[79]

People came to Jesus in increasing numbers until there was a great

[78] Matthew 15:29-31; Mark 7:31-37
[79] Matthew 15:32-39; Mark 8:1-10

multitude with nothing to eat. Jesus called his disciples, and said, "I have compassion on the people, because they have stayed with me now three days, and have nothing to eat. If I send them away to their home without food, they will faint on the way, for some of them have come a great distance."

His disciples answered him, "How could these people find bread in this deserted place?"

He asked them, "How many loaves do you have?"

They said, "Seven."

He commanded the multitude to sit down on the ground, and he took the seven loaves. Having given thanks, he broke them, and gave them to his disciples to serve, and they served the multitude. They also had a few small fish. Having blessed them, he said to serve these as well. The people, numbering about four thousand, ate and were filled. Afterward, the disciples gathered up seven baskets of broken pieces that were left over. Then he sent them away.

Faced with feeding another multitude, the disciples still didn't understand what Jesus intended. This time the obstacle was not lack of money, but lack of any place where food could even be bought. In what way is this situation like that of a refugee camp in our own day? Does God assist the efforts of those who go to great lengths to deliver supplies in seemingly impossible situations? Does it make a difference if those seeking to help refugees are following Jesus or not?

Prayer: How wonderful it is, Lord, when you make a way where there seems to be no way.

Thinking Like Pharisees[80]

Jesus entered into the boat with his disciples, and came into the region of Dalmanutha. They had forgotten to bring more bread, and had only one loaf in the boat with them. Jesus warned them: "Beware the yeast of the Pharisees and the yeast of Herod."

They said to one another, "It's because we have no bread."

Jesus, seeing their confusion, said, "Why do you think it's because you have no bread? Do you still not understand? Is

Even after seeing a multitude fed, the disciples were anxious about their food supply. They had failed to grasp one of Jesus' main points: God will provide. Can you think of examples in your own life when God provided for your needs in an amazing way? Even with what God has done for you, do you still find it difficult to trust when times are hard?

Prayer: Help me always remember, Lord, the way you have provided for me time and time again.

[80] Matthew 16:5-12; Mark 8:13-21

your heart still hardened? Having eyes, don't you see? Having ears, don't you hear? Don't you remember? When I broke the five loaves among the five thousand, how many baskets full of broken pieces did you take up?"

They told him, "Twelve."

"When the seven loaves fed the four thousand, how many baskets full of broken pieces did you take up?"

They told him, "Seven."

He asked them, "Don't you understand yet?"

Healing a Blind Man[81]

He came to Bethsaida. They brought a blind man, and begged Jesus to touch him. He took hold of the blind man's hand, and led him out of the village. When he had spit on his eyes, and laid his hands on him, he asked if he saw anything.

He looked up, and said, "I see men; they are like trees walking."

Then again he laid his hands on his eyes. The man was restored, and saw everyone clearly. Jesus sent him away to his house, saying, "Don't enter into the village, nor tell anyone in the village."

This is the only example of a partial healing by Jesus; a second touch was needed before the healing was complete. Have you ever been anxious for a quick fix of a problem which ended up requiring more time than you expected? Is it easier for you to counsel patience for others than to practice it in your own life?

Prayer: Give me patience, Lord, when answers to my problems don't come as quickly as I would like.

---

[81] Mark 8:22-26

Chapter 6: On to Jerusalem

The Transfiguration[82]

About eight days after these sayings, Jesus took with him Peter, John, and James, and went up onto the mountain to pray. As he was praying, the appearance of his face was altered, and his clothing became white and dazzling. Moses and Elijah, in radiant glory, spoke with him of what would happen at Jerusalem.

Peter and those with him were sound asleep, but when they woke up, they saw Jesus in his glory, and the two men who stood with him.

Peter said to Jesus, "Rabbi, it is good for us to be here. Let's make three tents: one for you, one for Moses, and one for Elijah." He didn't know what else to say because they were very afraid.

A cloud came, overshadowing them, and a voice came out of the cloud, "This is my beloved Son. Listen to him."

Suddenly they saw no one with them anymore, except Jesus. As they were coming down from the mountain, he commanded them to tell no one what they had seen until after the Son of Man had risen from the dead. They kept this saying to themselves, wondering what "rising from the dead" meant.

His disciples asked, "Why do the scribes say Elijah must come first?"

Jesus answered, "Elijah indeed comes first, and will restore all things, but I tell you Elijah has come already, and they

---

This marks a major turning point in the story of Jesus. Up until this time, Jesus has been teaching, healing and talking about God's kingdom. Now the story turns darker as Jesus sets his face toward Jerusalem and the fate that awaits him there. Have you ever had a sense of foreboding? Have you ever gone into a dark time in your life knowing God would be with you as you went through it?

Prayer: Help me be faithful, Lord, when dark and difficult times come.

---

[82] Matthew 17:1-13; Mark 9:2-13; Luke 9:28-36

didn't recognize him, but did to him whatever they wanted. The Son of Man will also suffer by them." Then the disciples understood he spoke to them of John the Baptizer.

Healing a Tormented Boy[83]

Later a crowd gathered around the disciples as scribes were questioning them. When everyone saw Jesus, they excitedly ran to him and greeted him. He asked the scribes, "What are you asking them?"

One of the crowd answered, "Teacher, I brought you my son, who has a mute spirit that causes seizures; he foams at the mouth, grinds his teeth, and wastes away. I asked your disciples to cast it out, and they weren't able."

He answered him, "Unbelieving generation, how long shall I bear with you? Bring him to me."

They brought him to Jesus, and when he saw him, the spirit convulsed the boy, and he fell on the ground, wallowing and foaming at the mouth.

He asked his father, "How long has it been since this began?"

He said, "From childhood. Often it has cast him into fire or water, to destroy him. If you can do anything, have compassion on us, and help."

Jesus said, "If you can believe, all things are possible to him who believes."

The father of the child cried out with tears, "I believe. Help my unbelief!"

When Jesus saw that a crowd was gathering, he rebuked the unclean spirit, saying to him, "You mute and deaf spirit, I command you, come out of him, and never enter him again!"

Having cried out, and convulsed greatly, it came out of him. The boy became like one dead, so much that most of them said, "He is dead." But Jesus took him by the hand, and raised him up.

The disciples asked Jesus privately, "Why weren't we able to cast it out?"

Prayer and fasting are prerequisites to the exercise of healing power; the more we are connected to God, the easier it is for God's healing power to flow through us. Do you believe God's healing power can flow through you? What are you doing to deepen your connection with God?

Prayer: Draw me closer to you, Lord, and let the healing power of your love flow through me.

---

[83] Matthew 17:14-21; Mark 9:14-29; Luke 9:37-43; Luke 17:5-6

He said to them, "Because of your unbelief. For most certainly I tell you, if you have faith as a grain of mustard seed, you will tell this mountain, 'Move from here to there,' and it will move; and nothing will be impossible for you. But this kind doesn't go out except by prayer and fasting."

Death and Taxes[84]

While everyone was marveling at the things Jesus did, he said to his disciples, "Let these words sink into your ears, for the Son of Man is being handed over to the hands of those who will kill him; and when he is dead, on the third day he will rise again." They didn't understand this saying. Its meaning was hidden to them, and they were afraid to ask him about it.

When they had come to Capernaum, those who collected the temple tax came to Peter, and said, "Doesn't your teacher pay the tax?" He said, "Yes."

When he came into the house, Jesus said, "What do you think, Simon? From whom do the kings of the earth receive toll or tribute? From their children, or from strangers?"

Peter said to him, "From strangers."

Jesus said to him, "Therefore the children are exempt. But, lest we cause them to stumble, go to the sea, cast a hook, and take the first fish that comes. When you open its mouth, you will find a coin. Take that, and give it to them for us."

There is a definite irony in Jesus paying the temple tax now and later driving out of the temple the people involved in collecting the tax. Such actions show ambivalence toward what the temple represented, not so different from the ambivalence many feel toward church today. How do you view church? What about church do you find disappointing or upsetting? What about it do you find meaningful?

Prayer: Lead us, Lord, to be the kind of church you would have us be.

Evaluating Behavior[85]

He came to Capernaum, and in the house he asked the disciples, "What were you talking about among yourselves on the way?"

They were silent, because they had argued about who was the greatest.

He sat down, called the twelve, and said, "Whoever wants to be first,

84 Matthew 17:22-27; Mark 9:30-32; Luke 9:43-45

85 Matthew 10:42; 18:1-9; Mark 9:33-50; Luke 9:46-50; 14:34-35; 17:1-2

shall be last of all, and servant of all." He took a little child, and set the child in their midst. Taking the child in his arms, he said, "Whoever receives one such little child in my name, receives me, and whoever receives me, receives him who sent me."

John said to him, "Teacher, we saw someone who doesn't follow us casting out evil spirits in your name; and we told him to stop, because he doesn't follow us."

Jesus said, "Don't forbid him, for there is no one who does a mighty work in my name will be able to quickly speak evil of me. Whoever is not against us is on our side. Those who give you a cup of water to drink in my name, because you are my followers, will in no way lose their reward.

If you cause one of these little ones who believe in me to stumble, it would be better for you to have a millstone hung around your neck, and be sunk in the depths of the sea.

"Woe to the world for the occasions of stumbling! Occasions must come, but woe to the person through whom they come! If your hand or your foot causes you to stumble, cut it off, and cast it from you. It is better for you to enter into life crippled, than to have both hands and both feet but be cast into the eternal fire.

When viewed from a kingdom perspective, much in life looks different: humility is the key to greatness; enemies are to be loved, not hated; sin is attractive, but destructive. Have your values and attitudes been changed by what Jesus says about God's kingdom? Who or what has played the biggest role in shaping your values?

Prayer: Deliver me, Lord, from living my life in accordance with the world's dehumanizing values.

Lost and Found[86]

See that you don't despise one of these little ones, because in heaven their angels always have the attention of my Father. The Son of Man came to save what was lost.

"What do you think? If a man has one hundred sheep, and one of them goes astray, doesn't he leave the ninety-nine, go to the mountains, and seek the one who is lost?

When he has found it, he carries it on his shoulders, rejoicing. When he comes home, he calls together his friends and his neighbors, saying to them, 'Rejoice with me, for I have found my sheep which was lost!' He

[86] Matthew 18:10-14; Luke 15:1-10

rejoices over it more than over the ninety-nine which have not gone astray.

Even so it is not the will of your Father in heaven that even one of these little ones should perish. There will be more joy in heaven over one sinner who repents, than over ninety-nine righteous people who need no repentance.

Or what woman, if she had ten silver coins, if she lost one coin, wouldn't light a lamp, sweep the house, and seek diligently until she found it? When she has found it, she calls together her friends and neighbors, saying, 'Rejoice with me, for I have found the coin which I had lost.' Even so, I tell you, there is joy in the presence of the angels of God over one sinner repenting."

One of the most common scenes in stained glass windows shows Jesus, the Good Shepherd, carrying the lost sheep. It is a great reminder that God cares not only for the multitudes, but for each person, including "the least of these." Are there people you tend to think of as being unimportant and easy to ignore? Are there people who think of you that way?

Prayer: Open the eyes of my heart, Lord, to see the infinite value you place on every life.

A Father's Love[87]

He said, "A certain man had two sons. The younger of them said, 'Father, give me my share of your property.' He divided his wealth between them. Not many days later, the younger son took everything he had and traveled into a far country, where he wasted his fortune in riotous living. When he had spent all of it, there arose a severe famine, and he became desperate. He went to work for a local farmer who sent him into his fields to feed pigs. He wanted to fill his belly with the husks that the pigs ate, but wasn't allowed.

When he came to himself, he said, 'My father's servants have bread enough to spare, and I'm dying of hunger! I will get up, go to him, and say, "Father, I have sinned against heaven, and against you. I am no longer worthy to be called your son. Make me as one of your hired servants."'

"He arose, and went to his father. But while he was still far off, his father saw him, and was moved with compassion; the father ran, fell on his neck, and kissed him. The son said, 'Father, I have sinned against heaven, and against you. I am no longer worthy to be called your son.'

"But the father said to his servants, 'Bring out the best robe, and put

[87] Luke 15:11-32

it on him. Put a ring on his hand, and shoes on his feet. Bring the fattened calf, kill it, and let us eat, and celebrate; for this, my son, was dead, and is alive again. He was lost, and is found.' They began to celebrate.

"Now his elder son was in the field. As he came near to the house, he heard music and dancing. He called one of the servants to him, and asked what was going on. He said to him, 'Your brother has come, and your father has killed the fattened calf, because he has received him back safe and healthy.'

The elder son was angry, and would not go in. His father came out, and begged him. But he answered his father, 'These many years I have served you. I never disobeyed a commandment of yours, but you never gave me even a goat, that I might celebrate with my friends. But when this son of yours came home after spending your money on prostitutes, you killed the fattened calf for him.'

"The father said, 'Son, you are always with me, and all that is mine is yours. But it was appropriate to celebrate and be glad, for this, your brother, was dead, and is alive again. He was lost, and is found.'"

Jesus told this parable, not to emphasize the son's sinfulness, but on the father's love. This is one of the central stories by which Jesus revealed the extravagance of God's love for those caught up either in rebellion against God or in self-righteous piety. In this story, do you identify more with one son than the other? In what way does this story speak of God's love for you?

Prayer: Thank you, Lord, for showing so clearly that God can love me even if the way I have lived fills me with shame.

The Importance of Forgiveness[88]

"If your brother sins against you, go, show him his fault between you and him alone. If he listens to you, you have gained back your brother. But if he doesn't listen, take one or two more with you, that at the word of two or three witnesses every accusation may be established. If he refuses to listen to them, tell it to the assembly. If he refuses to hear the assembly also, let him be to you as a Gentile or a tax collector.

If two agree on earth concerning anything they ask, it will be done for them by my Father in heaven. For where two or three are gathered together in my name, I am there in the middle of them."

Then Peter came and said to him, "Lord, how often shall I forgive someone who sins against me? Seven times?"

[88] Matthew 18:15-35; Luke 17:3-4

Jesus said to him, "Not seven times, but seventy times seven.

The kingdom of God is like a king who wanted to settle accounts with his servants. As he began, one was brought who owed ten thousand gold talents. Because he couldn't pay, his lord commanded him to be sold, with his wife, his children, and all that he had, and payment to be made. The servant knelt before him, saying, 'Lord, have patience with me, and I will repay you all!' The lord of that servant, being moved with compassion, released him, and forgave the debt.

"But that servant went out, and found one of his fellow servants, who owed him one hundred days wages, and he grabbed him, and took him by the throat, saying, 'Pay me what you owe!'

"His fellow servant fell down at his feet and begged him, 'Have patience with me, and I will repay you!' But he wouldn't, and cast him into prison until he should pay back what was due.

One of the sad facts of human nature is how resistant we can be to forgiving others even after we've experienced forgiveness ourselves. Do you find yourself falling into the trap of imagining you deserve to be forgiven while others don't? Do you tend to call your sins "mistakes" while seeing malicious intent in what others do?

Prayer: Help me show grace to others, Lord, in the extravagant way you have shown it to me.

When his fellow servants saw what was done, they were distraught, and came and told their lord. His lord called him in, and said, 'You wicked servant! I forgave your debt because you begged me. Shouldn't you have had mercy on your fellow servant, as I had mercy on you?' He delivered the man to the jailers, until he should pay all that was due. So my heavenly Father will do to you, if you don't forgive each other from your hearts."

Preparing for Jerusalem[89]

As the days went by, Jesus moved toward Jerusalem, and sent messengers on before him to a village of the Samaritans to prepare for his arrival. They didn't welcome him, though, because he was focused on Jerusalem. When his disciples, James and John, saw this, they said, "Lord, do you want us to command fire to come down from the sky, and destroy them, just as Elijah did?"

But he turned and rebuked them, and they went to another village.

[89] Matthew 19:1-2; Mark 10:1; Luke 9:51-56; 10:1-12, 17-20

The Lord appointed seventy others, and sent them two by two ahead of him into every city and place, where he was about to come. Then he said to them, "The harvest is indeed plentiful, but the laborers are few. Pray therefore to the Lord of the harvest, that he may send out laborers into his harvest. Go your ways. Behold, I send you out as lambs among wolves. Carry no purse, nor wallet, nor sandals. Greet no one on the way. Into whatever house you enter, first say, 'Peace be to this house.' If a person of peace is there, your peace will come to rest, but if not, it will return to you. Remain in that same house, eating and drinking the things they give, for the laborer is worthy of his wages. Don't go from house to house. Into whatever city you enter which receives you, eat what is set before you; heal the sick, and tell them, 'God's kingdom has come near to you.' But into any city you enter which doesn't receive you, go out into its streets and say, 'Even the dust from your city that clings to us, we wipe off against you. But know this: God's kingdom has come near you.' I tell you, it will be more tolerable for Sodom in the Day of Judgment than for that city.

Though Jesus felt drawn by destiny to Jerusalem, where people of violence would demand his death, he sent out a large group of his disciples to look for people of peace. Are you a person of peace, welcoming those who come with a message of peace? How do you live in peace as the world becomes ever more hostile and violent?

Prayer: Help me be a person of peace, Lord, in an angry, hateful world.

The seventy returned with joy, saying, "Lord, even the evil spirits are subject to us in your name!"

He said to them, "I saw Satan fall like lightning from heaven. I have given you authority to tread on serpents and scorpions, and over all the power of the enemy. Nothing will in any way hurt you. Nevertheless, don't rejoice that the spirits are subject to you, but rejoice that your names are written in heaven."

The Great Commandment[90]

One of the scribes came, and listened to their questions. Knowing that Jesus had answered them well, he asked, "Which commandment is the greatest of all?"

Jesus answered, "The greatest is, 'Hear, Israel, the Lord our God, the Lord is one: you shall love the Lord your God with all your heart, and

[90] Matthew 22:34-40; Mark 12:28-34; Luke 10:25-28

with all your soul, and with all your mind, and with all your strength.' This is the first and greatest commandment. The second is, 'You shall love your neighbor as yourself.' There is no commandment greater than these."

The scribe said to him, "Truly, teacher, you have said well that God is one, and there is no other; to love God with all the heart, and with all the understanding, with all the soul, and with all the strength, and to love your neighbor as yourself, is more important than all burnt offerings and sacrifices."

When Jesus saw that he answered wisely, he said, "You are not far from God's kingdom." After that, no one else dared ask any question.

The laws of Moses included not only the Ten Commandments, but more than six hundred other laws as well. Each one of these laws was scrutinized to determine exactly what was prohibited and what was allowed. Jesus said this multitude of laws could be summed up like this: love God and your neighbor. How do you measure up against this simple standard? Do you find it harder to love God or your neighbor?

Prayer: Keep reminding me, Lord, that endlessly analyzing the law is no substitute for following it.

The Good Samaritan[91]

But the man, desiring to justify himself, asked, "Who is my neighbor?"

Jesus answered, "A man going down from Jerusalem to Jericho fell among robbers, who stripped him and beat him, leaving him half dead. By chance a priest was going down that way; when he saw the man, he passed by on the other side. In the same way a Levite, when he saw the man, passed by on the other side. But a Samaritan, as he traveled, came where the man was. When he saw him, he was moved with compassion, and came to him, binding up his wounds, and pouring oil and wine on them. Then he put the man on his own animal, and brought him to an inn, and took care of him. On the next day, when he departed, he took out two day's wages, and gave them

Those who heard this story in Jesus' day would have been shocked, not by the actions of the Priest and the Levite, but that any Samaritan could be cast in the role of a hero. If Jesus were speaking to the church today, this might be the story of 'The Good Muslim,' or 'The Good Transgendered Person.' How would that change the story for you?

Prayer: When I think of loving my neighbor, Lord, remind me it may well be someone who is not much like me.

[91] Luke 10:29-37

to the host, saying, 'Take care of him. Whatever you spend beyond that, I will pay you when I return.' Now which of these three do you think was a neighbor to him who fell among the robbers?"

He said, "The one who showed mercy to him."

Then Jesus said to him, "Go and do likewise."

Hearing and Doing[92]

As they went on their way, he entered a village where a woman named Martha received him into her house. Her sister, Mary, sat at Jesus' feet, listening to what he said. Martha, distracted with serving, came up to him, and said, "Lord, don't you care that my sister left me to serve alone? Ask her to help me."

Jesus answered her, "Martha, Martha, you are anxious and troubled about many things, but one thing is needed. Mary has chosen the good part, which will not be taken away from her."

Mary's persistence in listening to Jesus was not to be set aside simply because Martha needed help doing what she felt obligated to do. There are times when customs, traditions and rules must be set aside in order to seize the moment. If you had no duties or obligations at this point in your life, what would you most want to do?

Prayer: Help me know the difference, Lord, between seizing the moment and shirking responsibilities.

He said to them, "Suppose you go to a friend at midnight, and say, 'Friend, lend me three loaves of bread, for someone has come to me from a journey, and I have no food to offer,' and the friend answers, 'Don't bother me. The door is shut, and my children and I are in bed. I can't get up and give it to you.' Although your friend won't rise and give it to you out of friendship, because of your persistence, your friend will get up and give you as much as you need.

As Jesus said these things, a woman in the crowd lifted up her voice, and said, "Blessed is the womb that bore you, and the breasts which nursed you!"

Jesus replied, "On the contrary, blessed are those who hear the word of God, and do it."

The Rich Fool[93]

One of the crowd said, "Teacher, tell my brother to divide the

---

[92] Luke 10:38-42; 11:5-8; 11:27-28

[93] Luke 12:13-21

inheritance with me."

But he said to him, "Man, who made me a judge or an arbitrator over you?" He said to the people, "Beware! Keep yourselves from greed, for life doesn't consist in the abundance of possessions."

He told them a parable: "The ground of a rich man produced abundantly. He thought to himself, 'What will I do? I don't have room to store my crops!' Then he decided, 'This is what I'll do. I'll pull down my barns, and build bigger ones, and there I will store all my grain and my goods. I will tell my soul, "You have many goods laid up for years to come. Take your ease, eat, drink, and be merry."'

"But God said to him, 'You fool! Tonight your soul is required of you. The things which you have prepared—whose will they be?' So it is with those who lay up treasure for themselves, and are not rich toward God."

The saying of Jesus, "Life does not consist in the abundance of possessions," is as true now as it was in his day, and yet many Christians show no evidence of having gotten the message. Who do you know who has consciously chosen to live a simple life based on lasting values? What would need to change in your life for you to live more simply?

Prayer: Set me on the right track, Lord, when I am tempted to pursue what promises much and delivers little.

Watchfulness and Faithfulness[94]

"Let your clothes be fastened and your lamps burning. Be like those watching for their master, when he returns from the marriage feast; when he comes and knocks, they immediately open to him. Blessed are those servants, whom the lord will find watching when he comes. He will see to his own needs while telling them to rest; then he will come and serve them. They will be blessed if he comes in the middle of the night, and finds them waiting.

But know this, if the master of the house had known when the thief was coming, he would have watched, and not allowed his house to be broken into. Be ready, because the Son of Man is coming in an hour you don't expect."

Peter said to him, "Lord, are you telling this parable to us, or to everybody?"

---

[94] Matthew 24:37-51; Luke 12:35-48

Jesus said, "Who then is the faithful and wise steward, given responsibility to see that everyone in the household has enough to eat? Blessed is the servant found carrying out his duties when his master returns. That servant will be given even greater responsibility. But if the servant says in his heart, 'My lord delays his coming,' and begins to beat the servants, and to eat and drink, and become drunk, then the lord of that servant will come in a day and hour when he isn't expected, and will cut him to pieces and put him with the unfaithful. That servant who knew what the master wanted and didn't even start to do it, will be beaten severely, but the servant who didn't know, and did evil things, will be beaten lightly. To whom much is given, much will be required; to whom much is entrusted, more will be asked.

Being a follower of Jesus is more a matter of responsibility than of privilege. These parables emphasize the importance of being ready when called any time of day or night. Have you ever had a job for which you were on call? Does following Jesus feel like that? Should it?

Prayer: Help me not become so comfortable, Lord, that I become presumptuous of what you would have me do.

The Fig Tree's Reprieve[95]

He told this parable. "A man had a fig tree planted in his vineyard, and he came seeking fruit on it, and found none. He said to the vine dresser, 'These three years I have come looking for fruit on this fig tree, and found none. Cut it down. Why should it be allowed to waste the soil?' He answered, 'Lord, leave it alone one more year while I dig around it, and fertilize it. If it bears fruit, fine; but if not, after that, you can cut it down.'"

This is a message that could be preached in many of our churches today. When God comes looking for fruit from your church, do you have more to offer than committee reports? If your church had one more year to become fruitful, what would you need to do first?

Prayer: Help me, Lord, do my part in helping the church bear fruit and not just consume resources.

There were some who told him about the Galileans, whose blood Pilate had murdered in the midst of their religious services. Jesus said, "Do you think these Galileans were worse sinners than all the other Galileans, because they suffered such things? No, but unless you repent, you will all perish the

[95] Luke 13:1-9

same way. Or those eighteen on whom the tower in Siloam fell and killed them: do you think they were worse offenders than all who dwell in Jerusalem? No, but unless you repent, you will all perish the same way."

Missing Out on the Kingdom[96]

Jesus was teaching in a synagogue on the Sabbath day when he saw a woman who had been crippled for eighteen years, bent over and unable to straighten herself up. Jesus said, "Woman, you are freed from your infirmity." He laid his hands on her, and immediately she stood up straight, and praised God.

The ruler of the synagogue, being indignant because Jesus had healed on the Sabbath, said to the multitude, "There are six days in which men ought to work. Therefore come on those days and be healed, and not on the Sabbath day!"

Jesus answered him, "You hypocrites! Doesn't each of you free your ox or your donkey from the stall on the Sabbath, and lead your animal to water? Shouldn't this woman, a daughter of Abraham bound by Satan eighteen long years, be freed from her bondage on the Sabbath day?"

As he said these things, his adversaries were disappointed, but the crowd rejoiced for the glorious things that were done by him.

He went on his way through cities and villages, teaching, and traveling on to Jerusalem. One follower said to him, "Lord, are there only a few who are saved?"

He said, "Strive to enter by the narrow door, for many will seek to enter and be unable. When the master has shut the door, and you stand outside and knock, saying, 'Master, open to us!' he will answer, 'I don't know you or where you come from.' You will say, 'We ate and drank in your presence, and you taught in our streets.' He will say, 'I don't know where you come from. Depart from me, you workers of iniquity.' There will be weeping and gnashing of teeth, when you see Abraham, Isaac, Jacob, and the prophets in God's kingdom, and you are thrown

These are harsh words of Jesus aimed at those whose lives are lacking in love and compassion, but who feel entitled to be part of God's kingdom. How has your faith made you a more loving person? In what situations do you find it most difficult to show love and compassion?

Prayer: Keep me from trying to shut people out of your kingdom, Lord, and being shut out myself in the process.

---

[96] Luke 13:10-17,22-30

outside. People will come from everywhere and will sit down to feast in God's kingdom. Some who are last will be first, and some who are first will be last."

Lament for Jerusalem[97]

That same day some Pharisees came, saying, "Get out of here right now because Herod wants to kill you."

He said to them, "Go and tell that fox, 'Behold, I will cast out evil spirits and heal people today and tomorrow; on the third day I will complete my mission. I must continue my journey these three days, because prophets always die in Jerusalem.

"Jerusalem, Jerusalem, who kills the prophets, and stones those who are sent to her! How often I would have gathered your children together, even as a hen gathers her chicks under her wings, and you would not let me! Your house is left to you desolate. You will not see me from now on, until you say, 'Blessed is he who comes in the name of the Lord!'"

Jesus was often criticized for the compassion he showed. It was not only the religious leaders who were upset with him, but political leaders like Herod as well. Have you ever been criticized for doing what you believed was right? Have you ever been critical of others and later come to realize they were doing what God led them to do?

Prayer: Give me courage to do the right thing, Lord, even when people are likely to be upset with me for it.

Humble Hospitality[98]

When he went into the house of one of the rulers of the Pharisees on a Sabbath to eat, many were watching him. Seeing a man who had dropsy, Jesus said to the lawyers and Pharisees, "Is it lawful to heal on the Sabbath?"

But they were silent.

He took the man, healed him, and let him go. He said, "Which of you, if your son or an ox fell into a well, wouldn't immediately pull him out on a Sabbath day?"

They couldn't answer him.

He told a parable to those who were invited, when he noticed how they chose the best seats: "When you are invited to a marriage feast,

---

[97] Matthew 23:37-39; Luke 13:31-35
[98] Luke 14:1-14

don't sit in the best seat, since someone more esteemed than you might be invited, and the one who invited both of you would come an d tell you, 'Make room for this person.' Then you would begin, with shame, to take the lowest place. But when you are invited, go and sit in the lowest place, so that the one who invited you may say, 'Friend, move up higher.' Then you will be honored in the presence of all who sit at the table with you. For those who exalt themselves will be humbled, and those who humble themselves will be exalted."

He also said to the one who had invited him, "When you give a dinner, don't invite your friends, your relatives, or your rich neighbors, because they might return the favor and pay you back. But when you have a feast, ask the poor, the maimed, the lame, or the blind. You will be blessed; they don't have the means to repay you, but you will be repaid in the resurrection of the righteous."

Rarely do those who insist the Bible must be taken literally have parables like these about humility and hospitality in mind. How would your life be different if you acted like this? What would it look like for a church to practice radical hospitality?

Prayer: Help me take seriously, Lord, the things you taught which challenge me the most.

God's Kingdom Feast[99]

When one of those who sat at the table with him heard these things, he said to him, "Blessed are those who will feast in God's kingdom!"

Jesus said to him, "A man had a great feast, and invited many people. When the time came, he out a servant to tell those who were invited, 'Come, everything is ready now.' But they all began to make excuses.

"The first said, 'I've bought a field, and must go see it. Please excuse me.'

"Another said, 'I've bought five yoke of oxen, and must go try them out. Please excuse me.'

"Another said, 'I've married a wife, and therefore I can't come.'

"The servant came, and told his lord these things. Then the master of the house was angry, and said to his servant, 'Go out quickly into the streets and lanes of the city, and bring in the poor, the crippled, the blind, and the lame.'

[99] Matthew 22:1-14; Luke 14:15-24

Who do you identify most with in this story? Do you make excuses when God calls you to do something? Are you one of the outcasts surprised to be invited to God's party?

Prayer: Touch my heart with the warmth of your love, Lord, that I might be truly excited by your invitation and presence.

"The servant said, 'Lord, it is done as you commanded, and there is still room.'

"The lord said to the servant, 'Go out into the highways and hedges, and compel them to come in, that my house may be filled. For I tell you that none of those invited will taste of my supper.'"

Costly Discipleship[100]

Large crowds were going with him. He turned and said to them, "If you come to me, and don't disregard your own father, mother, spouse, children, brothers, sisters, and, yes, your very own life, you can't be my disciple. Unless you bear your own cross, and come after me, you can't be my disciple. Which of you, desiring to build a tower, doesn't first sit down and count the cost, to see if you have enough to complete it? Or perhaps, when you have laid a foundation, and are not able to finish, everyone who sees begins to mock you, saying, 'This one began to build, and wasn't able to finish.' Or what king, as he goes to encounter another king in war, will not sit down first and consider whether he is able with ten thousand to meet him who comes against him with twenty thousand? Or else, while the other is yet a great way off, he sends an envoy, and asks for conditions of peace. So unless you renounce all you have, you can't be my disciple.

Like some of Jesus' other sayings, these words are not so much hard to understand as hard to follow. We are more familiar with a kind of "easy believism" in many churches: if you accept the church's beliefs, provide financial support, and attend worship you will be a good Christian. Is this the kind of commitment you've made? What would need to happen for you to make a deeper commitment to be a disciple?

Prayer: Show me, Lord, what holds me back from becoming what you have created me to be.

The Dishonest Manager[101]

He said to his disciples, "There was a certain rich man who had a manager. An accusation was made to him that this man was wasting his possessions. He called him, and said, 'What is this I hear about you? Give

---

100 Luke 14:25-33
101 Luke 16:1-9

an accounting because you can no longer be manager.'

"The manager said to himself, 'What will I do, seeing that my lord is taking away my position? I don't have strength to dig and am ashamed to beg. I know what I'll do, so that when I lose my job, others will welcome me into their homes.' Calling each of the debtors, he said to the first, 'How much do you owe my lord?' He said, 'A hundred barrels of oil.' He said to him, 'Take your bill, and quickly write down fifty.' Then he said to another, 'How much do you owe?' He said, 'A thousand bushels of wheat.' He said to him, 'Take your bill, and write eight hundred.'

It is hard to imagine an employer commending an employee for being smart in the way he cheated him. Perhaps the message here is to live a selfish life so that when everything falls apart (and it most likely will), you'll be ready to turn to God. Do you know anyone who is dishonest, but happy? Does ill-gotten gain ever truly enrich us?

Prayer: Deliver me, Lord, from foolishly thinking I can get to where I want to go in life by taking shortcuts.

"His lord commended the dishonest manager because he had done wisely. The children of this world are, in their own way, wiser than the children of the light. Make friends by means of wealth while you can, so that when you fail, you may be received into an eternal home.

The Importance of Faithfulness[102]

He who is faithful in a very little will be faithful also in much. He who is dishonest in a very little will also be dishonest in much. If you haven't been faithful with worldly wealth, who will entrust you with true riches? If you have not been faithful in what is another's, who will give you what is your own? No one can serve two masters, for either you will hate the one, and love the other; or else hold to one, and despise the other. You aren't able to serve God and wealth."

Here's what Jesus says: money and possessions are unimportant; people are important. How does your life measure up by these values? Have you resisted the lure of consumerism and materialism?

Prayer: Show me, Lord, what is truly important that I might not waste my life in trivial pursuits.

The Pharisees, who were lovers of money, heard these things and scoffed at him. He said to them, "You justify yourselves in the sight of people, but God knows your hearts. What is exalted in the world is detestable to God. The law and the

[102] Luke 16:10-17

prophets were primary until John. From that time on, the good news of God's kingdom has been preached, and people are trying to force their way in.

Rich Man and Lazarus[103]

"There was once a rich man, clothed in purple and fine linen, living in luxury every day. A beggar named Lazarus lay at his gate, full of sores and desiring to be fed with the crumbs that fell from the rich man's table. Yes, even the dogs came and licked his sores. The beggar died, and was carried away by angels to Abraham's bosom. The rich man also died, and was buried. In the torment of Hades, he lifted up his eyes and saw Abraham far off and Lazarus at his bosom. He cried, 'Father Abraham, have mercy on me, and send Lazarus, to dip the tip of his finger in water, and cool my tongue! For I am in anguish in this flame.'

"But Abraham said, 'Son, remember in your lifetime, you received good things, and Lazarus, in the same way, bad things. Now he is comforted here and you are in anguish. Between us and you there is a great chasm; those who want to pass from here to you are unable, and no one may cross over from there to us.'

"He said, 'I ask you, father, to send him to my father's house to warn my five brothers, so they won't also come to this place of torment.'

"But Abraham said, 'They have Moses and the prophets. Let them listen to them.'

"He said, 'No, father Abraham, but if one goes to them from the dead, they will repent.'

"He said to him, 'If they don't listen to Moses and the prophets, neither will they be persuaded if one rises from the dead.'"

The rich man had been unfaithful to God and unloving to his neighbor. Even in torment, the man had trouble seeing Lazarus as anything other than someone who could be his servant. Do you find this story disturbing? Who are the "beggars at the gate" most likely to be ignored today?

Prayer: Help me remember, Lord, that serving the poor is my simple duty, not something for which I should expect to be honored.

Who among you, having a servant plowing or keeping sheep, will say when the servant comes in from the field, 'Come now and sit down at the table,' but will rather say, 'Prepare my supper, clean up, and serve me, while I eat and drink. Afterward you shall eat and drink'? Does he thank the servant for doing what was required? I think not. Even so you also,

[103] Luke 16:19-31; 17:7-10

when you have done all the things commanded, should say, 'We are unworthy servants. We have only done our duty.'"

Cleansing Ten Lepers[104]

On his way to Jerusalem, Jesus traveled along the borders of Samaria and Galilee. As he entered a village, ten men who were lepers met him, and stood at a distance, crying out, "Jesus, Master, have mercy on us!"

When he saw them, he said, "Go and show yourselves to the priests." As they went, they were cleansed. One of them, when he saw he was healed, turned back, praising God loudly. He knelt before Jesus, thanking him; and he was a Samaritan. Jesus said, "Weren't there ten cleansed? Where are the nine? Did none return to give glory to God except this stranger?" Jesus said to him, "Get up. Go your way. Your faith has healed you."

The cleansing of ten lepers was a sign of God's kingdom. Another sign was the fact that one of the lepers was a Samaritan who came back to give God thanks. God's kingdom was for all people, not just for Jews. Do you have trouble seeing God's grace and true faith in other religious traditions? Who do you see as Samaritans (people of 'wrong' religions) in our own world?

Prayer: Thank you, Lord, for the breadth of your grace and the depth of your kingdom.

Being asked by the Pharisees when God's kingdom would come, he answered them, "God's kingdom doesn't come with observation; neither will they say, 'Look, it is here!' or, 'Look, it is there!' because God's kingdom is in your midst."

The Reprobate Judge[105]

He also spoke a parable to them that they must always pray and not give up, saying, "There was a judge in a certain city who didn't fear God, and didn't respect anyone. A widow in that city often came to him, saying, 'Defend me from my adversary!' He wouldn't for a while, but afterward he said to himself, 'Though I neither fear God, nor respect anyone, yet because this widow bothers me, I will

Will God, who can be counted on to be more responsive than a cranky judge, find faith and faithfulness, or fear and whining, when he comes to us? Are you more likely to respond to the day's news with fear or faith? What things in the community, nation or world bring out the worst in you?

Prayer: Help me live, Lord, in a way that expresses faith rather than fear.

---

104 Luke17:11-21
105 Luke 18:1-8

defend her. Otherwise she will wear me out by her persistence.'"

The Lord said, "Listen to what the unrighteous judge says. Won't God avenge his chosen ones, who are crying out to him day and night? He delays his response, but will avenge them soon. When the Son of Man comes, though, will he find faith?"

The Pharisee and the Tax Collector[106]

He spoke this parable to those who were convinced of their righteousness, and despised all others. "Two men went into the temple to pray; one was a Pharisee, and the other a tax collector. The Pharisee stood and prayed to himself like this: 'God, I thank you, that I am not like others: extortionists, unrighteous, adulterers, or even like this tax collector. I fast twice a week. I give tithes of all that I get.' But the tax collector, standing far away, wouldn't even lift his eyes to heaven, but beat his breast, saying, 'God, be merciful to me, a sinner!' I tell you, this man went down to his house justified rather than the other; those who exalt themselves will be humbled, and those who humble themselves will be exalted."

By saying true greatness finds its origin in humility, Jesus sets an almost impossible standard. Those who seek humility or any other goodness for the sake of their status in the eyes of others end up with self-righteousness and separation from God. True humility as seen in the prayer of the publican comes from brokenness. Where do you see yourself in this parable? Where does God see you?

Prayer: Deliver me, Lord, from the self-reflection which leads me to think my life is more righteous than that of others.

---

[106] Luke 18:9-14

Chapter 7: Judean Ministry

A Secret Trip to Jerusalem[107]

After these things, Jesus was traveling in Galilee, for he wouldn't go to Judea, because the Jews sought to kill him. The Feast of Booths was at hand and his brothers said to him, "Leave here and go to Judea that people there may see the works you do. No one should do such things in secret, but should seek to be known everywhere. If you do this, the whole world will know." (Even his brothers didn't believe in him.)

Jesus said to them, "My time has not yet come, but your time is always ready. The world doesn't hate you, but it hates me, because I tell how its works are evil. You go up to the feast. I'm not going up to this feast, because it isn't yet my time."

Having said these things to them, he stayed in Galilee. But when his brothers had left for the feast, he also went up, not publicly, but in secret. The Jews sought him at the feast, saying, "Where is he?" There was much murmuring among the crowds concerning him. Some said, "He is a good man." Others said, "No. He leads the multitude astray." Yet no one spoke openly of him for fear of the Jews.

It had become clear to Jesus that his ministry would bring him into conflict with religious and political authorities. He didn't run from this confrontation, but neither did he run to it. Instead, he waited until he had been assured by God that the time was right. Are you more likely to avoid conflict or embrace it? How do you decide when the time is right to do something you would rather avoid?

Prayer: Help me be bold, not foolish, Lord, when crises and conflicts come.

Teaching in the Temple[108]

In the middle of the feast, Jesus went to the temple and taught. The

107 John 7:1-13
108 John 7:14-39

Jews marveled, saying, "How does he know all of this, having never been educated?"

Jesus answered them, "My teaching is not mine, but his who sent me. Anyone who desires to do God's will knows whether my teaching is from God or if I am speaking for myself. Whoever speaks from himself seeks his own glory, but the one who seeks the glory of God is true, and no fault is in him. Didn't Moses give you the law, and yet none of you keeps the law? Why do you seek to kill me?"

The multitude answered, "You are crazy! Who seeks to kill you?"

Jesus answered them, "I did one sign, and you all marvel because of it. Moses gave you circumcision, and on the Sabbath you circumcise a boy. If a boy receives circumcision on the Sabbath to observe the law of Moses, are you angry with me because I healed a man on the Sabbath? Don't judge superficially, but judge rightly."

Some from Jerusalem said, "Isn't this the one our leaders seek to kill? He speaks openly, and yet they say nothing to him. Can it be that the rulers know this is truly the Christ? On the other hand, we know where this man comes from, but when the Christ comes, no one will know where he comes from."

Some of the people who listened to Jesus had a hard time making sense of what he said because it was at odds with their preconceived ideas. How open are you to new ideas? Do you latch onto the latest thing you've heard or resist anything that conflicts with what you've always believed? How do you recognize truth?

Prayer: Guide me, Lord, when new ways of thinking leave me uncertain whether to move forward or hold back.

Jesus spoke out in the temple, teaching and saying, "You know me, and know where I am from. I have not come of myself, but God who sent me is true. You don't know him, but I know him, because I am from him, and he sent me."

They wanted to take him, but no one laid a hand on him, because his hour had not yet come. Within the crowd, many believed in him. They said, "When the Christ comes, he won't do more signs than what this man has done, will he?" The Pharisees heard the multitude murmuring these things concerning him, and the chief priests and the Pharisees sent officers to arrest him.

Then Jesus said, "I will be with you a little while longer, then I go to him who sent me. You will seek me, and won't find me; and where I am, you can't come."

The Jews said among themselves, "Where will this man go that we won't find him? Will he go to the Dispersion among the Greeks, and teach the Greeks? What is this word that he said, 'You will seek me, and won't find me; and where I am, you can't come'?"

Now on the last and biggest day of the feast, Jesus stood and proclaimed, "If anyone is thirsty, let him come to me and drink! If you believe in me, as the Scripture has said, from within you will flow rivers of living water." He said this about the Spirit, which those believing in him were to receive. For the Holy Spirit was not yet given, because Jesus wasn't yet glorified.

Mixed Reactions[109]

Many of the crowd, when they heard these words, said, "This is truly the prophet." Others said, "This is the Christ." But some said, "What? Does the Christ come out of Galilee? Hasn't Scripture said the Christ comes from David, and from Bethlehem, David's village?" So there arose a division in the crowd because of him. Some wanted to arrest him, but no one did. The officers came to the chief priests and Pharisees, and said to them, "Why didn't you bring him in?"

The officers answered, "No man ever spoke like this man!"

The Pharisees answered them, "You aren't also led astray, are you? Have any of the rulers believed in him, or any of the Pharisees? This crowd is ignorant of the law and is accursed."

Nicodemus (the one who came to Jesus by night) said to them, "Does our law judge a man, unless it first hears from him personally and knows what he does?"

They answered him, "Are you also from Galilee? Search, and see that no prophet has arisen out of Galilee."

Some were convinced Jesus was the Messiah, while others thought he was an imposter because he didn't fit in with what they had always been told the Messiah would be. What has shaped your view of Jesus? Have you simply accepted everything you've been taught? How do you know if what you've been taught is true?

Prayer: Open my mind, Lord, to accept new ideas and to see you as you are and not simply as others have imagined you to be.

109 John 7:40-52

The Woman Caught in Adultery[110]

The others went to their houses, but Jesus went to the Mount of Olives. Very early in the morning, he came again to the temple, and people came to him. He sat down, and taught them. The scribes and the Pharisees brought a woman taken in adultery. Having set her in front of him, they said, "Teacher, we caught this woman in the very act of adultery. In our law, Moses commanded us to stone such women. What then do you say about her?" They said this to trap him that they might have a charge to bring against him.

Jesus stooped down, and wrote on the ground with his finger. When they continued asking him, he looked up and said to them, "Let the one without sin among you throw the first stone." Again he stooped down, and with his finger wrote on the ground.

When they heard it, being convicted by their conscience, they went out one by one, beginning from the oldest, until all were gone except Jesus and the woman. Standing up, Jesus said, "Woman, where are your accusers? Did no one condemn you?"

That this woman was "caught in the act" means the man should have been subject to stoning as well according to the law of Moses. Jesus turns the table on his accusers by making them face their hypocrisy. What is the worst injustice you have experienced? How did you react? How do you react to injustice suffered by others?

Prayer: Deliver me from hypocrisy, Lord, and give me the boldness to confront those who bully others.

She said, "No one, Lord."

Jesus said, "Neither do I condemn you. Go your way, and sin no more."

Light and Darkness[111]

Again Jesus spoke to the crowd, saying, "I am the light of the world. Whoever follows me will not walk in darkness, but will have the light of life."

The Pharisees said to him, "You talk about yourself. What you say isn't valid."

Jesus answered them, "Even if I talk about myself, my words are true, for I know where I came from, and where I'm going; you don't know

---

[110] John 7:53; John 8:1-11
[111] John 8:12-36

where I came from, or where I'm going. You judge according to the flesh. I judge no one, but if I do judge, my judgment is true, for I am not alone: I am with the Father who sent me. It's also written in your law that the testimony of two people is valid. I am one who testifies about myself, and the Father who sent me testifies about me."

They said therefore to him, "Where is your Father?"

Jesus answered, "You know neither me, nor my Father. If you knew me, you would know my Father also." Jesus spoke these words in the treasury, as he taught in the temple. Yet no one arrested him, because his hour had not yet come.

Jesus said again to them, "I am going away, and you will seek me, and you will die in your sins. Where I go, you can't come."

They said to one another, "Will he kill himself? He says, 'Where I'm going, you can't come'?"

He said to them, "You are from beneath. I am from above. You are of this world. I am not of this world. I said you will die in your sins, because unless you believe that I am the one, you will die in your sins."

They said to him, "Who are you?"

Jesus said to them, "Listen to what I've been saying to you from the beginning. I have many things to speak and to judge concerning you. He who sent me is true; the things which I heard from him, I say to the world."

They didn't understand that he spoke to them about the Father. Jesus said to them, "When you have lifted up the Son of Man, you will know that I am the one, and I do nothing of myself. As my Father taught me, I say these things. The one who sent me is with me. The Father hasn't left me alone, for I always do the things that are pleasing to him."

Jesus said several outrageous things about himself, claiming to be the light of the world and the truth that sets people free. If you heard someone say such things today, how would you react? Some said he was crazy; others said he was the real thing. What do you say?

Prayer: Give me wisdom to know the truth, Lord, and boldness to act on it.

As he spoke these things, many believed in him. Jesus said to those Jews who believed him, "If you remain in my word, then you are truly my disciples. You will know the truth, and the truth will make you free."

They answered him, "We are Abraham's offspring, and have never been in bondage to anyone. What do you mean by saying, 'You will be made free'?"

Jesus answered them, "Everyone who commits sin is a slave of sin. A slave doesn't live in the house, but the son does forever. If the Son makes you free, you will be free indeed.

Who You Are and Who I Am[112]

I know you are Abraham's offspring, yet you seek to kill me, because my word finds no place in you. I tell what I have seen with my Father; and you do what you have seen with your father."

They answered him, "Our father is Abraham."

Jesus said to them, "If you were Abraham's children, you would do the works of Abraham. But now you seek to kill me, a man who has told you the truth, which I heard from God. Abraham didn't do this. You do the works of your father."

They said, "We weren't born of sexual immorality. We have one Father, God."

Jesus said, "If God were your father, you would love me, for I came from God. I haven't come of myself, but he sent me. Why don't you understand what I say? It's because you can't listen. You are of your father, the devil, and you want to do the desires of your father. He was a murderer from the beginning, and doesn't stand in the truth, because there is no truth in him. When he speaks a lie, he speaks on his own, for he is a liar, and the father of lies. Because I tell the truth, you don't believe me. Which of you convicts me of sin? If I tell the truth, why don't you believe me? Whoever is of God hears the words of God. You don't hear, because you are not of God."

Then the Jews answered him, "Don't we say well that you are a Samaritan, and have an evil spirit?"

Jesus answered, "I don't have an evil spirit, but I honor my Father, and you dishonor me. But I don't seek my own glory. There is one who seeks and judges. Anyone who keeps my word will never see death."

Then the Jews said to him, "Now we know you have an evil spirit. Abraham died, and the prophets, yet you say, 'Whoever keeps my word will never taste of death.' Are you greater than our father, Abraham, who died? The prophets died. Who do you make yourself out to be?"

Jesus answered, "If I glorify myself, my glory is nothing. It is my Father who glorifies me, of whom you say that he is our God. You have

---

112 John 8:37-59

not known him, but I know him. If I said, 'I don't know him,' I would be like you, a liar. But I know him, and keep his word. Your father Abraham rejoiced to see my day. He saw it, and was glad."

The Jews therefore said to him, "You are not yet fifty years old, and have you seen Abraham?"

Jesus said to them, "I tell you, before Abraham came into existence, I am."

They took up stones to throw at him, but Jesus was hidden as he went out of the temple, passing by in their midst.

The Jewish leaders were claiming to be God's chosen people, but Jesus was claiming even more by saying he had come from God. The situation became intense as Jesus told them they were children of the devil, not children of Abraham. Do you see Jesus in this situation being harsh, angry and unfair? What do you think could have made him so upset? Do you get upset talking to people who don't agree with your religion?

Prayer: Give me holy boldness, Lord, tempered by love and humility.

Seeing and Not Seeing[113]

As he passed by, Jesus saw a man blind from birth. His disciples asked him, "Rabbi, who sinned, this man or his parents, that he was born blind?"

Jesus answered, "Neither this man sinned, nor his parents; this happened for the works of God to be revealed in him. I must do the work of him who sent me, while it is day. The night is coming, when no one can work. While I am in the world, I am the light of the world." When he had said this, he spat on the ground, made mud with the saliva, anointed the blind man's eyes with the mud, and said to him, "Go wash in the pool of Siloam." So he went away, washed, and came back seeing. The neighbors, and those who knew he was blind before, said, "Isn't this the one who sat and begged?" Others were saying, "It is he." Still others were saying, "It looks like him."

The man said, "I am he." They asked him, "How were your eyes opened?"

He answered, "A man called Jesus made mud, anointed my eyes, and said, 'Go to the pool of Siloam, and wash.' So I went and washed, and received my sight."

Then they asked him, "Where is he?"

He said, "I don't know."

They brought the man who had been blind to the Pharisees. It was a

---

[113] John 9:1-41

Sabbath when Jesus made the mud and opened his eyes. Again the Pharisees asked him how he received his sight. He said, "He put mud on my eyes, I washed, and I see."

Some of the Pharisees said, "This man is not from God, because he doesn't keep the Sabbath." Others said, "How can a man who is a sinner do such signs?" There was division among them. They asked the blind man again, "What do you say about him, because he opened your eyes?"

The man said, "He is a prophet."

The Jews did not believe the man had truly been blind and had received his sight until they called his parents and asked them, "Is this your son, whom you say was born blind? How then does he now see?"

His parents answered, "We know this is our son who was born blind, but how he now sees, or who opened his eyes, we don't know. He is of age. Ask him. He will speak for himself." His parents said these things because they feared the Jews who had already agreed that anyone who would confess Jesus as the Christ would be put out of the synagogue.

The Pharisees were interested in either disproving the miracle or discrediting the miracle worker. Neither approach worked very well. Are you skeptical by nature? Does it take a lot to convince you of something new? Is there any approach you've found effective in helping skeptics" see the light?"

Prayer: Open my eyes, Lord, that I not blindly resist what you are doing.

They called the man who was blind a second time, and said to him, "Give glory to God. We know this man is a sinner."

He answered, "I don't know if he is a sinner. One thing I do know: once I was blind, but now I can see."

They said to him again, "What did he do to you? How did he open your eyes?"

He answered them, "I told you already, and you didn't listen. Why do you want to hear it again? Do you also want to become his disciples?"

They insulted him and said, "You are his disciple, but we are disciples of Moses. We know that God has spoken to Moses. But as for this man, we don't know where he comes from."

The man answered them, "How amazing! You don't know where he comes from, yet he opened my eyes. We know that God doesn't listen to sinners, but listens to anyone who is a worshiper of God and does his will. Since the world began, no one has ever heard of someone opening the eyes of a man born blind. If this were not from God, he could do nothing."

They answered him, "You were totally born in sin, and you think you can teach us?" So they threw him out.

Jesus heard they had thrown him out, and finding him, said, "Do you believe in the Son of God?"

He answered, "Who is he, Lord, that I may believe in him?"

Jesus said to him, "You have seen him; it is he who speaks with you."

He said, "Lord, I believe!" and he worshiped him.

Jesus said, "I came into this world for judgment, that those who don't see may see; and that those who see may become blind."

Those of the Pharisees who were with him heard these things, and said to him, "Are we also blind?"

Jesus said to them, "If you knew you were blind, you would have no sin; but now you say, 'We see.' Therefore your sin remains.

The Good Shepherd[114]

"Anyone who doesn't enter by the door into the sheep fold, but climbs up some other way, is a thief and a robber. But one who enters by the door is the shepherd of the sheep. The gatekeeper opens the gate for him, and the sheep listen to his voice. He calls his own sheep by name, and leads them out. Whenever he brings out his own sheep, he goes before them, and the sheep follow him, for they know his voice. They will never follow a stranger, but will run away because they don't know the voice of strangers." Jesus spoke this parable to them, but they didn't understand what he was telling them.

This is such an intimate picture of a shepherd who knows and loves his sheep, calling each one by name and protecting them from all harm. The intimacy goes both ways because the sheep know the shepherd so well they will follow no one else. Does this image characterize your relationship with Jesus? Do you sense you are part of a flock or on your own?

Prayer: Help me recognize your voice clearly and follow you closely, Lord, trusting you to protect me always.

Jesus spoke to them again, "I tell you, I am the door for the sheep. All who came before me are thieves and robbers, but the sheep didn't listen to them. I am the door. If you enter in by me, you will be saved, and will go in and go out, and will find pasture. The thief only comes to steal, kill,

114 John 10:1-21

and destroy. I came that people may have life, and have it abundantly. I am the good shepherd. The good shepherd lays down his life for the sheep. A hired hand, who isn't a shepherd and doesn't own the sheep, sees a wolf coming, and runs away, leaving the sheep. The wolf snatches the sheep, and scatters them. The hired hand doesn't care about the sheep. I am the good shepherd. I know my own, and my own know me, even as the Father knows me, and I know the Father. I lay down my life for the sheep. I have other sheep also, which are not of this fold. I must bring them as well, and they will hear my voice. They will become one flock with one shepherd. The Father loves me, because I lay down my life, that I may take it again. No one takes it away from me, but I lay it down myself. I have power to lay it down, and I have power to take it again. I received this authority from my Father."

A division arose again among the Jews because of these words. Many of them said, "He has an evil spirit, and is insane! Why do you listen to him?" Others said, "These are not the sayings of one possessed by evil. It isn't possible for an evil spirit to open the eyes of the blind, is it?"

Family Matters[115]

Pharisees came to him, testing him by saying, "Is it lawful for a man to divorce his wife for any reason?"

He answered, "Haven't you read that God who made them from the beginning made them male and female, and said, 'For this cause a man shall leave his father and mother, and shall join to his wife; and the two shall become one flesh?' What God has joined together, no one should tear apart."

They asked him, "Why then did Moses command us to give her a bill of divorce, and leave her?"

He said to them, "Moses, because of the hardness of your hearts, allowed you to divorce your wives, but from the beginning it has not been so. Whoever divorces his wife, except for sexual immorality, and marries another, commits adultery; and whoever marries a divorced woman commits adultery."

His disciples said, "If this is the case of, it is better not to marry."

He said to them, "Not everyone can receive this saying, but only those to whom it is given. There are eunuchs who were born that way

[115] Matthew 19:3-15; Mark 10:2-16; Luke 18:15-17

from their mother's womb, and there are eunuchs who were made so by others; and there are eunuchs who made themselves so for the sake of God's kingdom. He who is able to receive it, let him receive it."

They began to bring little children to Jesus to touch them, but the disciples rebuked those who were bringing them. When Jesus saw it, he was moved with indignation, and said to them, "Allow the little children to come to me! Don't forbid them, for God's kingdom belongs to such as these. Whoever will not receive God's kingdom like a little child will in no way enter into it." He took the children in his arms, and blessed them, laying his hands on them.

In the world of Jesus' day, Jewish women had minimal rights. Divorce was quick and simple, could only be initiated by men, and could be done for any reason; divorced women were left with no property, no income and no way to support their children. What are some key factors in building a long-lasting and deeply satisfying marriage? Have you had opportunity to welcome and bless children as Jesus did?

Prayer: Thank you, Lord, for all the different kinds of families that evil demonstrate healthy relationships.

The Challenge of Wealth[116]

A man came to Jesus and said, "Good teacher, what shall I do that I may have eternal life?"

He said to him, "Why do you call me good? No one is good but God alone. If you want to enter into life, keep the commandments."

He said to him, "Which ones?"

Jesus said, "'You shall not murder.' 'You shall not commit adultery.' 'You shall not steal.' 'You shall not offer false testimony.' 'Honor your father and mother.' And, 'You shall love your neighbor as yourself.'"

The young man said to him, "All these commandments I have obeyed from my youth. What do I still lack?"

Jesus, looking upon him, loved him and said, "If you want to be complete, go and sell what you have; give to the poor, and you will have treasure in heaven; then come, follow me." When the young man heard this, he went away sad, for he was one who had great possessions.

Jesus looked around, and said to his disciples, "How difficult it is for those who have riches to enter into God's kingdom!"

---

116 Matthew 19:16-30; Mark 10:17-32; Luke 18:18-30

The disciples were amazed at his words. But Jesus said, "How hard is it for those who trust in riches to enter into God's kingdom! It is easier for a camel to go through a needle's eye than for the wealthy to enter God's kingdom."

They were astonished, saying to him, "Then who can be saved?"

Jesus, looking at them, said, "With people it is impossible, but not with God, for all things are possible with God."

Peter began to tell him, "We have left everything, and have followed you."

Jesus said, "There is no one who has left house, or family or land, for my sake, and for the sake of the good news, who will not receive one hundred times more in this time, with persecutions, and in the age to come eternal life. Many who are first will be last, and the last first."

The problem with wealth is the way people value it, seek it, serve it, and trust it rather than God. For the wealthy, God is often one thing among many in their lives; for the poor, God is the only thing they have. How seriously do you take these words of Jesus? Do you imagine they are intended for those who have far more wealth than you? Are there people who consider you to be wealthy?

Prayer: Help me not become so attached to things of this world, Lord, that I prefer them to you.

A Matter of Fairness[117]

"The kingdom of God is like a master of a household, who went out early in the morning to hire laborers for his vineyard. When he had agreed with the laborers for a day's wage, he sent them out to work. He went out about the third hour, and saw others standing idle in the marketplace, and said to them, 'You also go into the vineyard, and whatever is right I will pay you.' So they went their way. Again he went out about the sixth and the ninth hour, and did likewise. About the eleventh hour he went out, and found others standing idle. He said to them, 'Why do you stand here all day without working?'

"They said to him, 'Because no one has hired us.'

"He said to them, 'You also go into the vineyard, and you will be paid what is right.' When evening had come, the lord of the vineyard said to his manager, 'Call the laborers and pay them their wages, beginning from the last to the first.'

"When those who were hired at about the eleventh hour came, they each received a full day's wage. When the first came, they supposed that

[117] Matthew 20:1-16

they would receive more, but they received the same. They murmured against the master of the household, saying, 'These last have spent one hour, and you have made them equal to us, who have borne the burden of the day and the scorching heat!'

"But he answered them, 'Friends, I am doing you no wrong. Didn't you agree with me for a day's wage? Take that which is yours, and go your way. It is my desire to give to these just as much as to you. Isn't it lawful for me to do what I want to with what I own? Or is your eye evil because I am good?' So the last will be first, and the first last. For many are called, but few are chosen."

The grace of God is not an easy matter for us to grasp. Those who rejoice at being loved unconditionally themselves often become angry when others are shown grace. People who heard this story in Jesus' day probably didn't like it any better than people today. How do you react when some are given better than they deserve? Do you find it difficult to show grace to others?

Prayer: Show me a gracious way to celebrate the blessings of others, Lord, whenever become envious.

Tell Us Plainly Who You Are[118]

It was the Feast of the Dedication at Jerusalem. It was winter, and Jesus was walking in Solomon's porch in the temple. The Jews came around him and said, "How long will you hold us in suspense? If you are the Christ, tell us plainly."

Jesus answered, "I already told you, and you don't believe. The works I do in my Father's name testify about me. You don't believe because you are not of my sheep, as I told you. My sheep hear my voice, and I know them, and they follow me; I give eternal life to them. They will never perish, and no one will snatch them out of my hand. My Father, who has given them to me, is greater than all. No one is able to snatch them out of my Father's hand. I and the Father are one."

The Jews took up stones again to kill him. Jesus said, "I have shown you many good works from my Father. For which of those works do you stone me?"

They answered him, "We don't stone you for a good work, but for blasphemy: because you, being a man, make yourself God."

Jesus answered, "Isn't it written in your law, 'I said, you are gods?' If he called them gods, to whom the word of God came (and Scripture can't be broken), do you say of the one the Father sent into the world, 'You

---

[118] John 10:22-42

blaspheme,' because I said, 'I am the Son of God?' If I don't do the works of my Father, don't believe me. But if I do them, even though you don't believe me, believe the works. That way you can know and believe the Father is in me, and I am in the Father."

When Jesus spoke clearly, the Jewish leaders recoiled in horror that anyone should dare speak such blasphemy. Some enter into dialogue honestly; others only listen to find ways to trip up their opponent. Are you more likely to dialogue with others or argue with them? How open are you to hearing what others think?

Prayer: Calm me down, Lord, when what others say brings out the worst in me.

They sought again to seize him, and he escaped from them.

He went away again beyond the Jordan into the place where John had first baptized, and stayed there. Many came to him, saying, "John did no signs, but everything John said about this man is true." Many believed in him there.

The Raising of Lazarus[119]

Lazarus, the brother of Martha and Mary of Bethany, was sick. The sisters sent to Jesus, saying, "Lord, the one you love is sick." When Jesus heard it, he said, "This sickness is not to death, but for the glory of God, that God's Son may be glorified." Jesus loved Martha, Mary, and Lazarus, but when he heard Lazarus was sick, he stayed two days where he was. After this he said to the disciples, "Let's go into Judea again."

The disciples told him, "Rabbi, the Jews were just trying to stone you. Are you going there again?"

Jesus answered, "Aren't there twelve hours of daylight? If you walk in the day, you don't stumble, because you see the light of this world. But if you walk in the night, you stumble, because the light isn't in you." After saying these things, he said to them, "Our friend, Lazarus, has fallen asleep, but I am going to wake him from his sleep."

The disciples said, "Lord, if he has fallen asleep, he will recover."

Jesus had spoken of his death, but they thought he spoke of sleeping. He said to them plainly, "Lazarus is dead. I am glad for your sakes I was not there, so that you may believe. Nevertheless, let's go to him."

Thomas said to his fellow disciples, "Let's go also, that we may die with him."

[119] John 11:1-44

When Jesus came, he learned Lazarus had been in the tomb four days already. Bethany was near Jerusalem, less than two miles away, and many of the Jews had joined the women around Martha and Mary, to console them about their brother. When Martha heard Jesus was coming, she went and met him, but Mary stayed in the house. Martha said to Jesus, "Lord, if you would have been here, my brother wouldn't have died. Even now I know whatever you ask, God will give you." Jesus said to her, "Your brother will rise again."

Martha said, "I know he will rise again in the resurrection at the last day."

Jesus said to her, "I am the resurrection and the life. Whoever believes in me will live, even after death. Whoever lives and believes in me will never die. Do you believe this?"

The tension in the story comes from Jesus not being there when Lazarus was sick and delaying his coming until after he had died. Have you ever been upset with God for something terrible that happened? In retrospect, can you see ways in which God was present and involved through it all?

Prayer: Open my eyes to see your presence in the darkest days, Lord, and know you are still at work.

She said to him, "Yes, Lord. I have come to believe that you are the Christ, God's Son, who comes into the world."

When she had said this, she went away, and called Mary, her sister, secretly, saying, "The Teacher is here, and is calling you."

When Mary heard, she rose quickly, and went to him. Jesus had not yet come into the village, but was in the place where Martha met him. The Jews in her house consoling her, when they saw Mary rise up and go out, followed her, saying, "She is going to the tomb to weep there." When Mary came to where Jesus was, she fell down at his feet, saying, "Lord, if you would have been here, my brother wouldn't have died."

When Jesus saw her weeping, and the Jews who came with her weeping, he groaned in his spirit, and was troubled, saying, "Where have you laid him?"

They told him, "Lord, come and see."

Jesus wept.

The Jews said, "See how much affection he had for him!" Some of them said, "Couldn't this man, who opened the eyes of the one who was blind, also have kept this man from dying?"

Jesus, again groaning in himself, came to the tomb, a cave with a stone against it. Jesus said, “Take away the stone.”

Martha said, “Lord, by this time there is a stench; he’s been dead four days.”

Jesus said to her, “Didn’t I tell you if you believed, you would see God’s glory?”

They took away the stone from the place where the dead man was lying. Jesus lifted up his eyes, and said, “Father, I thank you that you listened to me. I know that you always listen to me, but because of the crowd standing around I said this, that they may believe you sent me.” When he had said this, he cried with a loud voice, “Lazarus, come out!”

The one who was dead came out, bound hand and foot with wrappings, and his face wrapped with a cloth.

Jesus said to them, “Free him, and let him go.”

Religious Leaders Plot against Jesus[120]

When Jesus had finished all these words, he said to his disciples, “You know that after two days the Passover is coming, and the Son of Man will be delivered up to be crucified.”

Then the chief priests, the scribes, and the elders of the people were gathered together in the court of the high priest, who was called Caiaphas. They took counsel together that they might take Jesus by stealth, and kill him. But they said, “Not during the feast, lest a riot occur among the people.”

Many of the Jews who came to Mary and saw what Jesus did, believed in him, but some of them went away to the Pharisees, and told them what Jesus had done. The chief priests and the Pharisees gathered a council, and said, “What are we doing? This man does many signs. If we leave him alone, everyone will believe in him, and the Romans will come and take away our positions and our nation.”

Caiaphas, the high priest that year, said to them, “You know nothing at all, nor do you realize it is better for us that one man should die for the people, than the whole nation perish.” Now he didn’t say this of himself, but being high priest that year, he prophesied Jesus would die for the nation, and not for the nation only, but to gather into one the children of God who are scattered abroad. From that day forward they began to plan

[120] Matthew 26:1-5; Mark 14:1-2; John 11:45-57

for his death.

Jesus walked openly among the Jews no more, but departed into the country near the wilderness, to a city called Ephraim. He stayed there with his disciples.

The Passover was at hand and many went up from the country to Jerusalem to purify themselves. They looked for Jesus and spoke with each other as they stood in the temple, "What do you think? Isn't he coming to the feast at all?" The chief priests and the Pharisees had commanded anyone who knew where he was to report it, for them to seize him.

As Jesus became increasingly popular, the Jewish leaders focused on what they had to lose because of him rather than on what they had to gain. Those with power and privilege always act to maintain their positions. Can you think of modern day examples? If you were in a position of power today, would you see Jesus as a threat?

Prayer: Open my eyes, Lord, when my self-interest blinds me from seeing what is good and right for everyone.

Jesus Moves Forward[121]

The crowds were on the way, going up to Jerusalem. To their amazement, Jesus was in front of them; those who followed were afraid. He took the twelve aside, and began to tell them what was going to happen to him. "We are going up to Jerusalem. The Son of Man will be delivered to the chief priests and the scribes, who will condemn him to death, and deliver him to the Romans. They will mock him, spit on him, scourge him, and kill him. On the third day he will rise again."

They understood none of these things. This was all hidden from them, and they didn't understand what was said.

James and John, the sons of Zebedee, came near to him, saying, "Teacher, we want you to do for us whatever we will ask."

He said to them, "What do you want me to do for you?"

They said to him, "Grant to us that we may sit, one at your right hand, and one at your left hand, in your glory."

But Jesus said to them, "You don't know what you are asking. Are you able to drink the cup I drink, and be baptized in the way I will be?"

They said to him, "We are able."

[121] Matthew 20:17-28; Mark 10:32-45; Luke 18:31-34; 22:24-30

Jesus said, "You shall indeed drink the cup I drink, and be baptized in the way I will be, but to sit at my right hand and at my left is not mine to give."

When the ten heard it, they began to be indignant towards James and John.

Jesus summoned them, and said, "Those who are recognized as rulers over nations lord it over them, and their great ones exercise authority over them. It shall not be so among you: whoever wants to be great among you shall be your servant. Whoever wants to be first among you, shall be slave of all. The Son of Man came not to be served, but to serve, and to give his life as a ransom for many."

The contrast between Jesus and his disciples can be clearly seen here: Jesus was resolutely moving toward his destiny of sacrifice and service; the disciples were seeking positions of power and privilege. In three years with Jesus had they learned anything? In what ways has your life been shaped by a Christ-like call to sacrifice and service?

Prayer: Challenge my thinking, Lord, when I began to focus on my self-interest instead of your call on my life.

Blind Bartimaeus[122]

As Jesus came to Jericho with his disciples and a crowd, Bartimaeus, a blind beggar, was sitting by the road. When he heard that it was Jesus the Nazarene, he began to cry out, "Jesus, son of David, have mercy on me!" Many told him to be quiet, but he cried out much more, "Son of David, have mercy on me!"

Jesus stood still, and said, "Call him."

They called the blind man, saying to him, "Cheer up! Get up. He's calling you!"

Bartimaeus, casting away his cloak, sprang up, and came to Jesus.

Jesus asked him, "What do you want me to do for you?"

The blind man said to him, "Great Master, I want to see again."

Jesus said to him, "Go your way. Your faith has made you well." Immediately he received his sight, and followed Jesus on the way.

Everyone else saw the blind man who wouldn't be quiet as a nuisance; Jesus saw him as a child of God and a man of faith. How do you react when people complain and protest? What do you think you might hear if you asked what they wanted, as Jesus did with this man?

Prayer: Open my ears, Lord, to the cries of those the world tries to silence.

122 Matthew 20:29-34; Mark 10:46-52; Luke 18:35-43

Zacchaeus[123]

Jesus passed through Jericho, where Zacchaeus, a chief tax collector who was very rich, lived. He was trying to get a glimpse of Jesus, but couldn't because he was too short and the crowd was too great. Determined to see, he ran on ahead, and climbed into a sycamore tree to see Jesus as he passed that way. When Jesus came, he looked up and saw him, and said, "Zacchaeus, hurry and come down; I must stay at your house today." He came down quickly, and received Jesus joyfully. When the crowd saw it, they all murmured, saying, "Jesus has gone to the home of a man who is a sinner."

No one among the Jews was more reviled than tax collectors. As a chief tax collector, Zacchaeus would have been considered the worst of the worst, and yet Jesus wanted to see him as much as he wanted to see Jesus. Has your spiritual journey been one of you reaching out to God or of God reaching out to you? Have you experienced both happening at the same time?

Prayer: Thank you, Lord, for seeking me while I was seeking you.

Zacchaeus stood and said, "Lord, half of my goods I will give to the poor. If I have wrongfully taken anything from anyone, I will restore four times as much."

Jesus said, "Today, salvation has come to this house, because this man also is a son of Abraham. The Son of Man came to seek and to save that which was lost."

Parable of the Talents[124]

Jesus went on to tell them a parable: "It is like a man, going into another country, who called his servants, and entrusted his wealth to them. To one he gave five million, to another two million, to another one million, according to their ability. Then he went on his journey. The one who received five million went and traded with it, and made another five million. In the same way, the one who got the two gained another two. But the one who received one million went and dug a hole, and hid his lord's money.

"After a long time the lord of those servants came, and reconciled accounts with them. The first said, 'Lord, you gave me five million. I have gained five more.'

"His lord said, 'Well done, good and faithful servant. You have been

---

[123] Luke 19:1-10

[124] Matthew 25:14-30; Luke 19:11-27

faithful over a few things, I will set you over many things. Enter into the joy of your lord.'

"The second came and said, 'Lord, you gave me two million. I have gained another two million.'

"His lord said, 'Well done, good and faithful servant. You have been faithful over a few things, I will set you over many things. Enter into the joy of your lord.'

"The one who had received one million came and said, 'Lord, I knew you were a hard man, reaping where you didn't sow, and gathering where you didn't scatter. I was afraid, and hid your talent in the earth. Here is what you gave me.'

"His lord answered, 'You wicked and lazy servant. You knew I reap where I don't sow, and gather where I don't scatter. You ought to have deposited my money with bankers, and at my coming I would have received back my own with interest.' Take away the million from him, and give it to the one who has ten million. For to everyone who has will be given more in abundance, but from those who have little, even what they have will be taken away. Throw out the unprofitable servant into the outer darkness, where there will be weeping and gnashing of teeth.'

Considering that each talent was worth about $1 million in today's currency, these servants were entrusted with a lot of money! It is unclear whether the servant with one talent was motivated by fear or dishonesty, but clearly the master was upset by the lack of effort. How do you evaluate what you have done with the life God has given you? Do you expect "Well done, good and faithful servant" to be your reward?

Prayer: Help me do something, Lord, with the abilities and opportunities you've given me.

Anointed for a Funeral[125]

Six days before the Passover, Jesus came to Bethany, to the home of Lazarus, who had been raised from the dead. Jesus had supper there, with Martha serving, and Lazarus among those sitting at the table with him. Mary, took a pound of ointment of pure nard, very expensive, and anointed the feet of Jesus, and wiped his feet with her hair. The house was filled with the fragrance of the ointment. Then Judas Iscariot, the disciple who would betray him, said, "Why wasn't this ointment sold for a year's wages, and given to the poor?" He said this, not because he cared for the poor, but because he was dishonest, and stole from the money

[125] Matthew 26:6-13; Mark 14:3-9; John 12:1-11

box. Jesus said, "Leave her alone. She has kept this for the day of my burial. For you always have the poor with you, and you can help them whenever you want, but you don't always have me. Wherever this good news is preached in the whole world, what this woman has done will be spoken of as a memorial of her."

A large crowd of the Jews learned he was there, and they came, not for Jesus' sake only, but to see Lazarus as well, whom he had raised from the dead. The chief priests conspired to put Lazarus to death, because on account of him many of the Jews went away and believed in Jesus.

This is the only indication that Judas was dishonest, focused on worldly riches rather than spiritual ones. He begins at this point to separate himself from those who are devoted to Jesus, and align himself with those who seek the death of both Jesus and Lazarus. What makes people align themselves with forces of death and destruction? Have you ever been tempted to do so? Could you be?

Prayer: Don't let me get off track, Lord, and end up with those who oppose you.

Chapter 8: The Final Week

The Triumphal Entry[126]

When they came to the Mount of Olives near Jerusalem, he sent two of his disciples, and said to them, "Go into the village that is opposite you. As you enter, you will find a young donkey who no one has ridden. Untie him, and bring him. If anyone asks you, 'Why are you doing this?' say, 'The Lord needs him;' and he will send him back here."

They went away, and found a young donkey in the street, and they untied him. Some of those who stood there asked, "What are you doing, untying the donkey?" They said to them what Jesus had said, and they let them go.

Jesus' entry into Jerusalem symbolized peaceful revolution: 'peaceful' because he entered on a humble donkey rather than a powerful warhorse; 'revolution' because he allowed himself to be hailed as a Messiah who would save his people and inaugurate a kingdom. Do you see following Jesus to be a revolutionary act? In what way are you a peaceful revolutionary?

Prayer: Continue to challenge me, Lord, that I not take you for granted and miss out on your revolution.

They brought the young donkey to Jesus, and threw their garments on it, and Jesus sat on it. Many spread their garments on the way, and others were cutting down branches from the trees, and spreading them on the road. Those who went in front, and those who followed, cried out, "Hosanna! Blessed is he who comes in the name of the Lord! Blessed is the kingdom of our father David that is coming in the name of the Lord! Hosanna in the highest!"

This was to fulfill what was written, "Don't be afraid, daughter of Zion. Your King comes, sitting on a donkey's colt." His disciples didn't understand these things at first, but when Jesus was raised from the dead, they remembered what had been written about

126 Matthew 21:1-9; Mark 11:1-10; Luke 19:28-40; John 12:12-19

him. The crowd that was with him when he called Lazarus out of the tomb was talking about it. Others went and met him, because they heard that he had done this sign. The Pharisees said among themselves, "We've accomplished nothing; the whole world has gone after him."

Lament for Jerusalem[127]

The next morning, as Jesus returned to the city, he was hungry. Seeing a fig tree by the road, he came to it, and found nothing on it but leaves. He said to it, "Let there be no fruit from you forever!" The fig tree withered away.

As they passed by later, they saw the fig tree withered away from the roots. Peter said to him, "Rabbi, look! The fig tree you cursed has withered away."

Jesus answered, "Have faith in God. If you tell this mountain, 'Be taken up and cast into the sea,' and don't doubt in your heart, but believe it is happening, you shall have whatever you ask. Whatever you pray for, believe you have received it, and you shall have it. And whenever you pray, forgive anything you have against anyone, and your Father in heaven will also forgive your sins. But if you do not forgive, neither will your Father in heaven forgive you."

The miracles Jesus did had a purpose that was sometimes obvious and other times obscure. The cursed fig tree that bore no fruit was like the Jewish leaders in Jerusalem who refused to follow a path that would lead to peace. In the years since then, how much have we learned about peace? Does Jesus still weep over a world that believes wars bring peace? Do you consider yourself a pacifist?

Prayer: Remove my anger and need for vengeance, Lord, and help me be a person who works tirelessly for peace.

When he came near, he saw the city and wept over it, saying, "If you had only known what brings peace! But now, it is hidden from your eyes. The days will come when your enemies will throw up a barricade against you, hem you in on every side, and dash you and your children to the ground. They won't leave one stone unturned, because you didn't recognize the time of your visitation."

Cleansing the Temple[128]

When he had come into Jerusalem, all the city was stirred up, saying, "Who is this?" The crowds said, "This is the prophet, Jesus, from Nazareth

---

127 Matthew 21:18-22; Mark 11:11-14; 11:20-26; Luke 19:41-44
128 Matthew 21:10-27; Mark 11:15-33; 12:41-44; Luke 19:45-20:8; 21:1-4

of Galilee."

Jesus sat down opposite the temple, and saw how everyone put money into the treasury. Many who were rich put in much. A poor widow came, and put in two of the smallest coins. He said to his disciples, "This poor widow gave more than all the others; they gave out of their abundance, but she, out of her poverty, gave all she had."

Many of those who gave in the temple did so from questionable motives, and those who facilitated their offerings were absolutely corrupt. As Jesus sought to change this, he was accused of acting without the proper authority. Have you ever felt led to do something that proved unpopular to those in charge? Do you find it easy to stand up for yourself when accused of acting without proper authorization?

Prayer: Give me the boldness I need, Lord, when doing what you've called me to do upsets those in charge.

Jesus entered into the temple of God, and drove out all of those who sold and bought there, and overthrew the money changers' tables and the seats of those who sold the doves. He said to them, "It is written, 'My house shall be called a house of prayer,' but you have made it a den of robbers!"

The blind and the lame came to him in the temple, and he healed them. But when the chief priests and the scribes saw the wonderful things he did, and the children who were crying in the temple, "Hosanna to the son of David!" they were indignant, and said to him, "Do you hear what these are saying?"

Jesus said to them, "Yes. Did you never read, 'Out of the mouth of babes and toddlers you have brought praise?'"

He left them, and went out of the city to Bethany, and camped there.

They came again to Jerusalem, and as he was walking in the temple, the chief priests, scribes, and elders came to him and asked, "By what authority do you do these things? Who gave you this authority?"

Jesus said to them, "I will ask you one question. Answer me, and I will tell you by what authority I do these things. The baptism of John—was it from heaven, or from men? Answer me."

They reasoned with themselves, saying, "If we say, 'From heaven;' he will say, 'Why then didn't you believe him?' If we say, 'From men'" the people who believe John was a prophet will attack us." They answered Jesus, "We don't know."

Jesus said to them, "Neither do I tell you by what authority I do these things."

Parables of Faithfulness[129]

"What do you think? A man had two sons. He came to the first, and said, 'Son, go work today in my vineyard.' He answered, 'No,' but afterward he changed his mind, and went. He came to the second, and said the same thing. He answered, 'Yes, sir,' but he didn't go. Which of the two did the will of his father?"

They said to him, "The first."

Jesus said to them, "I tell you tax collectors and prostitutes are entering into God's kingdom before you. John came to you in the way of righteousness, and you didn't believe him, but the tax collectors and prostitutes believed him. When you saw it, you didn't even repent afterward, that you might believe him.

"Hear another parable. The master of a household planted a vineyard, set a hedge about it, dug a wine press in it, built a tower, leased it out to farmers, and went into another country. When the season came near, he sent his servants to the farmers to receive his fruit. The farmers took his servants, beat one, killed another, and stoned another. Again, he sent other servants, more than the first, and they treated them the same way. Afterward he sent to them his son, saying, 'They will respect him.' But the farmers, when they saw the son, said among themselves, 'This is the heir. Come, let's kill him, and steal his inheritance.' So they took him, and threw him out of the vineyard, and killed him. When therefore the lord of the vineyard comes, what will he do to those farmers?"

These stories were clear warnings to Jewish leaders that they would be held accountable for their failure to carry out God's mission of being a light to the world. Do you see these stories as clear warnings to Christian leaders of the same thing? How faithful has the church been in carrying out God's mission of being a light to the world?

Prayer: Point me to others, Lord, with whom I can join together in carrying your light into the darkness.

They told him, "He will utterly destroy those miserable wretches, and will lease out the vineyard to other farmers, who will give him the fruit in its season."

Jesus said to them, "Did you never read in the Scriptures,

'The stone which the builders rejected,
the same was made the cornerstone.

---

[129] Matthew 21:28-46; Mark 12:1-12; Luke 20:9-19

This was from the Lord.
It is marvelous in our eyes?'

"God's kingdom will be taken away from you, and will be given to those producing its fruit. Those who fall on this stone will be broken by it, but those on whom it falls, will be obliterated."

When the chief priests and the Pharisees heard his parables, they understood he spoke about them. They wanted to seize him, but they feared the crowds who considered him to be a prophet.

Trick Questions for Jesus[130]

They watched him, and sent out spies, who pretended to be righteous, that they might trap him in something he said in order to deliver him up to the power and authority of the governor. They asked him, "Teacher, we know that you say and teach what is right, and aren't partial to anyone, but truly teach the way of God. Is it lawful for us to pay taxes to Caesar, or not?"

But he perceived their craftiness, and said to them, "Why do you test me? Show me a coin. Whose image and inscription are on it?"

They answered, "Caesar's."

He said to them, "Then give to Caesar the things that are Caesar's, and to God the things that are God's."

Unable to trap him in his words before the people, they marveled at his answer, and were silent.

Some Sadducees, who deny there is a resurrection, came to Jesus and asked, "Teacher, Moses wrote to us that if a man's brother dies having a wife, and he is childless, his brother should take the wife, and raise up children for his brother. There were therefore seven brothers. The first took a wife, and died childless. The second took her as wife, and he died childless. The third took her, and likewise the seven all left no children, and died. Afterward the woman also died. In the

Sincere questions are important; trick questions are not. These questions came, not from a desire to understand, but from a desperation to undermine. What are some examples of sincere questions and trick questions people have today? Do your questions ever fall into the latter category?

Prayer: Keep me honest and sincere, Lord, when I struggle with my questions or those of others.

130 Matthew 22:15-33; Mark 12:13-27; Luke 20:20-40

resurrection whose wife will she be? For the seven had her as a wife."

Jesus said to them, "The children of this age marry, and are given in marriage, but those who are deemed worthy to attain to the age to come and resurrection from the dead, neither marry, nor are given in marriage. They can't die any more, for they are like the angels, and are children of God, being children of the resurrection. But that the dead are raised, even Moses showed at the bush, when he called the Lord 'The God of Abraham, the God of Isaac, and the God of Jacob.' Now he is not the God of the dead, but of the living, for all are alive to him."

Some of the scribes answered, "Teacher, you speak well." They didn't dare ask him any more questions.

Pointing Out Inconsistencies[131]

Now while the Pharisees were gathered together, Jesus asked them a question, saying, "What do you think of the Christ? Whose son is he?"

They said to him, "David's."

He said to them, "How then does David in the Spirit call him Lord, saying,

'The Lord said to my Lord,
sit on my right hand,
until I make your enemies a footstool for your feet?'

"If then David calls him Lord, how is he his son?"

No one was able to give any answer. From that day forward, no one dared ask him any more questions.

Then Jesus spoke to the crowds and his disciples, saying, "The scribes and the Pharisees sat on Moses' seat. Whatever they tell you to do, go ahead and do, but don't follow their example because they don't do what they say. They bind heavy burdens on others, but themselves will not lift a finger to help anyone. Everything they do is for the sake of appearances. They make their phylacteries broad, enlarge the fringes of their garments, and love the place of honor at feasts, the best seats in the synagogues,

The question Jesus asks the Pharisees here highlights a lack of consistency in how they used the scriptures. Then he contrasted what they practice and what they preach. Does this kind of hypocrisy continue to be a problem among believers? Do you expect more from others than you demand of yourself?

Prayer: Don't let me turn a blind eye, Lord, to hypocrisy in my life.

131 Matthew 22:41-46; 23:1-12; Mark 12:35-40; Luke 20:41-47

the salutations in the marketplaces, and to be called 'Rabbi, Rabbi' by men. Don't call anyone 'Rabbi,' for only the Christ is your teacher, and all of you are equals. Call no man on earth your father, for you have one Father in heaven. Neither be called masters, for only the Christ is your master. Whoever is greatest among you will be your servant.

Beware of the scribes, who like to walk in long robes, and to get greetings in the marketplaces, and the best seats in the synagogues, and the best places at feasts: they are the ones who devour widows' houses, and for a pretense make long prayers. They will receive greater condemnation."

Woe to the Scribes and Pharisees[132]

"Woe to you, scribes and Pharisees, hypocrites! You shut up the kingdom of God against others because you are unwilling to enter in yourselves or lend a hand to those who want to enter. Woe to you, scribes and Pharisees, hypocrites! You travel around by sea and land to make one convert, and whoever becomes one is twice the child of hell you are.

"Woe to you, you blind guides, who say, 'Swearing by the temple is nothing, but swearing by the gold of the temple is binding.' You blind fools! Which is greater, the gold, or the temple that sanctifies the gold? Or 'Swearing by the altar is nothing, but swearing by the gift on it is binding?' You blind fools! Which is greater, the gift, or the altar that sanctifies the gift? Whoever swears by the altar, swears by it, and by everything on it. Whoever swears by the temple, swears by it, and by God who is in it. Whoever swears by heaven, swears by the throne of God, and by the one who sits on it.

"Woe to you, scribes and Pharisees, hypocrites! For you tithe mint, dill, and cumin, and have left undone the weightier matters of the law: justice, mercy, and faith. You ought to have done the latter, without leaving the former undone. You blind guides, who strain out a gnat, and swallow a camel!

"Woe to you, scribes and Pharisees, hypocrites! For you clean the outside of the cup and the platter, but within you are full of extortion and unrighteousness. You blind Pharisee, first clean the inside of the cup and of the platter, that its outside may become clean also.

---

132 Matthew 23:13-36

"Woe to you, scribes and Pharisees, hypocrites! For you are like whitened tombs, which outwardly appear beautiful, but inwardly are full of skeletons, and all uncleanness. Even so you also outwardly appear righteous to men, but inwardly you are full of hypocrisy and iniquity.

"Woe to you, scribes and Pharisees, hypocrites! For you build the tombs of the prophets, and decorate the tombs of the righteous, and say, 'If we had lived in the days of our fathers, we wouldn't have acted with them in spilling the blood of the prophets.' You admit you are children of those who killed the prophets. And you live up to the heritage of your fathers. You serpents, you brood of vipers, how will you escape the judgment of hell? I will send to you prophets, wise men, and scribes. Some of them you will kill and crucify; some you will scourge in your synagogues, and persecute from city to city, that on you may come all the innocent blood shed on the earth, from the blood of righteous Abel to the blood of Zachariah, whom you killed between the sanctuary and the altar. I tell you plainly, all these things will come upon this generation.

Jesus was known for his embrace of the poor and outcast, and for his harsh words toward the religious leaders of his day. He was not so much upset with what they chose for themselves, but with the harm they did to others. Have you seen people in churches who leave a path of destruction behind them? Does your church find it difficult to confront those who hurt others in what they say and do?

Prayer: Help me be sensitive to the needs of those around me, Lord, and bold to confront those who do others harm.

The Coming Destruction[133]

As he went out of the temple, one of his disciples said to him, "Teacher, see how wonderful these stones and buildings are!"

Jesus said to him, "Do you see these great buildings? There will not be left here one stone on another, which will not be thrown down."

As he sat on the Mount of Olives opposite the temple, Peter, James, John, and Andrew asked him privately, "Tell us when these things will be? What is the sign they are all about to be fulfilled?"

Jesus began to tell them, "Be careful that no one leads you astray. For many will come in my name, saying, 'I am he! ' and will lead many astray.

"The days will come, when you will desire to see the day of the Son of Man, and you will not see it. They will tell you, 'Look, here!' or 'Look,

133 Matthew 24:1-31; Mark 13:1-27; Luke 17:22-37; 21:5-24

there!' Don't follow after them, for as the lightning, when it flashes out of one part under the sky to the other part under the sky, so will the Son of Man be in his day. But first, he must suffer many things and be rejected by this generation. As it was in the days of Noah, even so will it be also in the days of the Son of Man. They ate, they drank, they married, they were given in marriage, until the day Noah entered into the ship, and the flood came, and destroyed them all. It was the same in the days of Lot: they ate, they drank, they bought, they sold, they planted, they built; but in the day Lot went out from Sodom, it rained fire and sulfur from the sky, and destroyed them all. It will be the same way the day the Son of Man is revealed. In that day, he who will be on the housetop, and his goods in the house, let him not go down to get them. Let the one who is in the field not turn back. Remember Lot's wife! Those who seek to save their lives will lose them, but those who lose their lives will save them. In that night there will be two people in one bed: one will be taken, and the other left. There will be two grinding grain together: one will be taken, and the other left."

They asked him, "Where, Lord?"

He said to them, "Where the body is, there will the vultures also be gathered together."

"When you hear of wars and rumors of wars, don't be troubled. For those must happen, but the end is not yet. For nation will rise against nation, and kingdom against kingdom. There will be earthquakes in various places. There will be famines and troubles. These things are the beginning of birth pains.

"Family members will betray each other, causing them to be killed. You will be hated by all for my name's sake, but whoever endures to the end will be saved.

When you see the abomination of desolation, spoken of by Daniel the prophet, standing where it ought not (let the reader understand), then let those who are in Judea flee to the mountains, and let those who are on the housetop not go down, nor enter in, to take anything out of the house. Those who are in the field should not go back for their clothes. Woe to those who are with child and to those who nurse babies in those days! Pray that your flight won't be in the winter. In those days there will be trouble, such as has not been known from the days of creation until now, and never will be. Unless the Lord shortens the days, no one would be saved; but for the sake of the chosen ones, he shortens the days.

Then if anyone tells you, 'Look, here is the Christ!' or, 'Look, there!' don't believe it. For there will arise false christs and false prophets, who will show signs and wonders to lead astray, if possible, even the chosen ones. Be on your watch.

"I have told you all things now. In those days, after that tribulation, the sun will be darkened, the moon will not give its light, the stars will be falling from the sky, and the powers in the heavens will be shaken. They will see the Son of Man coming in clouds with great power and glory. He will send out his angels to gather his chosen ones from the four winds, from the ends of the earth to the sky.

Apocalyptic language like this can be hard to understand, particularly for those who don't realize much of it was fulfilled about thirty years later when Rome brutally crushed a Jewish rebellion and destroyed Jerusalem and the temple. The prophecies of stars falling from the sky is metaphorical language akin to our speaking of earth-shattering events. How familiar are you with the destruction of Jerusalem in 66 A.D.? It is almost impossible to understand the prophetic passages of the New Testament without knowing some history from that era.

Prayer: Help me understand, Lord, the portions of scripture that have already found their fulfillment in history.

Watch and Prepare[134]

"From the fig tree, learn this parable. When the branch has become tender, and produces its leaves, you know summer is near; even so, when you see these things coming to pass, know it is near. This generation will not pass away until all these things happen. Heaven and earth will pass away, but my words will not pass away. No one knows the day or hour, not even the angels in heaven, nor the Son, but only the Father. Watch, keep alert, and pray; you don't know when the time will come.

"It is like a man, traveling to another country, having left his house, and given authority to his servants, and to each one his work, and also commanded the doorkeeper to stay alert. Watch therefore, because you don't know when the lord of the house is coming, whether at evening or at midnight, or when the rooster crows, or in the morning. Otherwise, the master when coming might find you sleeping. What I tell you, I tell everyone: Watch."

"Be careful, or your hearts will be loaded down with carousing, drunkenness, and cares of this life, and the day will come on you suddenly. For it will come like a snare on all those who dwell on the

[134] Matthew 24:32-36; 25:1-13; Mark 13:28-37; Luke 21:25-38

earth. Be watchful all the time, praying that you may be counted worthy to escape all these things that will happen, and to stand before the Son of Man."

"The kingdom of God will be like ten virgins, who took their lamps, and went out to meet the bridegroom. Five of them were foolish, and five were wise. Those who were foolish, when they took their lamps, took no oil with them, but the wise took oil in their vessels with their lamps. While the bridegroom delayed, they all slept. At midnight there was a cry, 'Behold! The bridegroom is coming! Come out to meet him!' Then all the bridesmaids arose, and trimmed their lamps. The foolish said to the wise, 'Give us some of your oil, for our lamps are going out.' But the wise answered, 'What if there isn't enough for us and you? Go to those who sell, and buy for yourselves.' While they went away, the groom came, and those who were ready went in with him to the marriage feast, and the door was shut. Afterward the other bridesmaids also came, saying, 'Lord, Lord, open to us.' But he answered, 'Most certainly I tell you, I don't know you.' Watch, for you don't know the day nor the hour in which the Son of Man is coming.

It is easy to be either oblivious to the return of Christ or obsessed by it. The important thing is not to have figured out the date (which is impossible), but to be ready whenever it might be. None of us has a guarantee of when either our lives or our world will end. How often do you think of the end of your life? Is it possible to prepare for the unexpected?

Prayer: Help me live each day fully, Lord, faithful to you for however many days I have on this earth.

The Last Judgment[135]

"When the Son of Man comes, and all the angels with him, he will sit on the throne of his glory. Before him all the nations will be gathered, and he will separate them one from another, as a shepherd separates the sheep from the goats. He will set the sheep on his right hand, and the goats on the left. Then the King will tell those on his right hand, 'Come, blessed of my Father, inherit the kingdom prepared for you from the foundation of the world; for I was hungry, and you gave me food to eat. I was thirsty, and you gave me drink. I was a foreigner, and you took me in. I was naked, and you clothed me. I was sick, and you visited me. I was in prison, and you came to me.'

[135] Matthew 25:31-46

"Then the righteous will answer him, saying, 'Lord, when did we see you hungry, and feed you; or thirsty, and give you a drink? When did we see you as a foreigner, and take you in; or naked, and clothe you? When did we see you sick, or in prison, and come to you?'

"The King will answer them, 'Whenever you did it to one of the leas t of these, you did it to me.' Then he will say also to those on the left hand, 'Depart from me, you cursed, into the eternal fire which is prepared for the devil and his angels; for I was hungry, and you didn't give me food to eat; I was thirsty, and you gave me no drink; I was a foreigner, and you didn't take me in; naked, and you didn't clothe me; sick, and in prison, and you didn't visit me.'

"Then they will also answer, saying, 'Lord, when did we see you hungry, or thirsty, or a foreigner, or naked, or sick, or in prison, and didn't help you?'

"Then he will answer them, 'Whenever you didn't do it to one of the least of these, you didn't do it to me.' They will go away into eternal punishment, but the righteous into eternal life."

Jesus says we will be judged, not on what we believe, but on how we live out our faith by having compassion on the poor in our midst. Jesus identifies fully with "the least of these," saying what happens to them happens to him. Where do you see yourself in this judgment scene? Do your priorities and those of your church line up with what Jesus says here?

Prayer: When I become like the world around me and turn my back on the poor, Lord, remind me that to do so is to turn my back on you.

Reflections on Death[136]

There were a number of Greeks among the Jews who went up to worship at the feast. They came to Philip, who was from Bethsaida of Galilee, and said, "Sir, we want to see Jesus." Philip came and told Andrew, and in turn, Andrew came with Philip, and they told Jesus. Jesus answered them, "The time has come for the Son of Man to be glorified. Unless a grain of wheat falls into the earth and dies, it remains by itself alone. But if it dies, it bears much fruit. Those who love their lives will lose them. Those who hate their lives in this world will keep them to eternal life. Whoever serves me, must follow me. Where I am, there will my servant also be. The Father will honor anyone who serves me.

"My soul is troubled. Shall I say, 'Father, save me from this time?' It is for this purpose I came to this time. Father, glorify your name!"

---

[136] John 12:20-36

Jesus speaks here of his death, but not of his death only. Dying to self and coming alive in God is central to the teaching of Jesus and contrary to almost everything in the world. What does it mean to you to die to self? Is it an event? A process? What does it involve?

Prayer: In the mystery of dying to self, Lord, help me grab hold of the life that is truly worth living.

A voice from the heavens said, "I have glorified it, and will glorify it again." The crowd who stood by and heard said it had thundered. Others said, "An angel has spoken to him."

Jesus answered, "This voice hasn't come for my sake, but for yours. Now is the judgment of this world. Now the prince of this world will be cast out. If I am lifted up from the earth, I will draw all people to myself." He said this, signifying how he would die. The crowd answered, "We have heard from the law that the Christ remains forever. How do you say, 'The Son of Man must be lifted up?' Who is this Son of Man?"

Jesus therefore said to them, "Yet a little while the light is with you. Walk while you have the light, so that darkness doesn't overtake you. Whoever walks in the darkness doesn't know where he is going. While you have the light, believe in the light, that you may become children of light." Jesus said these things and left, hiding himself from them.

Explaining Unbelief[137]

Though Jesus had done so many signs in their presence, there were many who didn't believe in him. This fulfilled the word of Isaiah the prophet,

"Lord, who has believed our report?
To whom has the arm of the Lord been revealed?"

For this cause they couldn't believe, for Isaiah said again,

"He has blinded their eyes and hardened their heart,
lest they should see with their eyes,
and perceive with their heart,
and would turn,
and I would heal them."

Isaiah said these things when he saw his glory, and spoke of the Christ. Many believed in him, even among the rulers, but because of the Pharisees they didn't confess it. Loving praise from others rather than

137 John 12:37-50

from God, they feared being put out of the synagogue. Jesus cried out and said, "Whoever believes in me, believes not in me, but in him who sent me. Whoever sees me sees him who sent me. I have come as a light into the world, that whoever believes in me may not remain in the darkness. Whoever listens to my sayings, and doesn't believe, is not judged by me. I came not to judge the world, but to save the world. Whoever rejects me, and doesn't receive my sayings, is judged by the word that I spoke, because I spoke not from myself, but from the Father who sent me. He gave me a word to speak, and I know his word is eternal life. The things I say are what the Father has said to me."

Exodus 7-14 speaks both of God hardening Pharaoh's heart and of Pharaoh hardening his own heart. The same idea is expressed here: unbelief can be used by God, even if not caused by God. How do you see belief and unbelief at work in your own life? Is God pulling you one way or another, or are these choices you are making on your own?

Prayer: Be at work in my life, Lord, drawing me ever closer to you.

Passover Preparations[138]

As Passover was approaching, the chief priests and scribes sought how they might put Jesus to death, for they feared the people. Satan entered into Judas Iscariot, one of the twelve. He went away, and talked with the chief priests and captains about how he might deliver him to them. They were pleased, and agreed to pay him. He began to look for an opportunity to deliver him to them in the absence of the crowd.

The day of unleavened bread came on which Passover is observed. He sent Peter and John, saying, "Go and prepare the Passover for us, that we may eat."

They said to him, "Where do you want us to prepare?"

He said to them, "When you have entered into the city, a man carrying a pitcher of water will meet you. Follow him into the house which he enters. Tell the master of the house, 'The Teacher says to

Passover was the central, defining celebration in Jewish life because it commemorated their liberation from slavery in Egypt centuries before. In Egypt, they had been told to kill a lamb and put its blood on the doorpost of each house. God said, "When I see the blood, I will pass over *you and your house." In this way the Hebrews were spared the death that came upon the Egyptians. How do you react to this story? Do you know Jewish families who still celebrate this today?*

Prayer: Help me understand, Lord, that deliverance from evil always comes at a price.

138 Matthew 26:1-5,17-18; Mark 14:10-17; Luke 22:1-14

you, "Where is the guest room, where I may eat the Passover with my disciples?"' He will show you a large, furnished upper room. Make preparations there."

They went, found things as he had told them, and prepared the Passover. When the hour had come, he sat down with the twelve.

Washing the Disciples' Feet[139]

Knowing his time had come to return to the Father, and having loved his own who were in the world, Jesus now loved them to the end even as the devil put into the heart of Judas Iscariot to betray him. Knowing that the Father had given all things into his hands, and that he came from God, and was returning to God, Jesus arose from supper, laid aside his outer garments, took a towel and wrapped it around his waist. Then he poured water into the basin, and began to wash the disciples' feet, and to wipe them with the towel. He came to Simon Peter, who said to him, "Lord, do you wash my feet?"

Jesus answered, "You don't know what I am doing now, but you will understand later."

Peter said to him, "You will never wash my feet!"

Jesus answered him, "If I don't wash you, you have no part with me."

Simon Peter said, "Lord, not my feet only, but also my hands and my head!"

Jesus said to him, "Someone who has bathed only needs to have his feet washed to be completely clean. You are clean, but not all of you." For he knew the one who would betray him, therefore he said, "You are not all clean." So when he had washed their feet, put his outer garment back on, and sat down again, he said to them, "Do you know what I have done to you? You rightly call me, 'Teacher' and 'Lord,' for so I am. If I then, your Lord and Teacher, have washed your feet, you also ought to wash one another's feet. I have given you an example that you also should do as I have done to you. A servant

In a time and place where roads were dusty and travel was on foot, it was customary for a host to have a servant wash the feet of house guests. By washing his disciples' feet, Jesus set a powerful model of humble service, fully consistent with the transformed values of God's kingdom. What lowly task in our own day might be compared to foot washing? In what way has Jesus' example served as a model for you?

Prayer: Keep reminding me, Lord, that no act of service to a person in need is beneath me.

[139] John 13:1-20

is not greater than his lord, neither is one who is sent greater than the one who sent him. If you know these things, blessed are you if you do them. I don't speak concerning all of you. I know whom I have chosen; the Scripture will be fulfilled, 'He who eats bread with me has lifted up his heel against me.' From now on, I tell you before it happens, that when it happens, you may believe I am he. Whoever receives someone I send, receives me; whoever receives me, receives the one who sent me."

Foreseeing Betrayal[140]

When Jesus had said this, he was troubled in spirit, and said, "One of you will betray me."

The disciples looked at one another, perplexed about whom he spoke. John was at the table, leaning against Jesus' breast. Simon Peter beckoned to him, and said, "Tell us who it is of whom he speaks."

Leaning as he was on Jesus' breast, John asked, "Lord, who is it?"

Jesus answered, "It is the one to whom I will give this piece of bread when I have dipped it." So when he had dipped the piece of bread, he gave it to Judas, the son of Simon Iscariot. After the piece of bread, Satan entered into him.

Jesus said to him, "What you do, do quickly."

No one at the table knew why he said this to him. Some thought, because Judas had the money box, that Jesus said to him, "Buy what things we need for the feast," or that he should give something to the poor. Having received the morsel, Judas went out immediately into the night.

When he had gone out, Jesus said, "Now the Son of Man has been glorified, and God has been glorified in him. If God has been glorified in him, God will also glorify him in himself, and he will do so soon. Little children, I will be with you a little while longer. You will seek me, and as I said to the Jews, 'Where I am going, you can't come,' so now I tell you. A new commandment I give you that you love one another. Just as I have loved you, you also love one

Jesus knew he would be betrayed and who would betray him, but none of the others did. It is tempting to imagine Judas as the ultimate villain, but that is not the way the disciples saw him. Have you ever been surprised to discover the dark side of someone you respected and admired? How aware are you of your own dark side?

Prayer: Keep me honest, Lord, that I might never imagine evil of others without imagining it of myself as well.

[140] Matthew 26:21-25; Mark 14:18-21; Luke 22:21-23; John 13:21-35

another. By this everyone will know you are my disciples, if you have love for one another."

The Last Supper[141]

He said to them, "I have earnestly desired to eat this Passover with you before I suffer, for I tell you, I will not eat it again until it is fulfilled in God's kingdom." He received a cup, and when he had given thanks, he said, "Take this, and share it among yourselves, for I tell you, I will not drink again from the fruit of the vine, until God's kingdom comes."

He took bread, and when he had given thanks, he broke it and gave to them, saying, "This is my body which is given for you. Do this in memory of me." Likewise, he took the cup after supper, saying, "This cup is the new covenant in my blood, which is poured out for you."

This meals was by invitation only, but not exclusive in the usual sense: Jesus invited those who would betray, deny and abandon him. He knew them well and invited them anyway. What does the Last Supper mean to you? Do you feel connected to Jesus and those who follow him when you participate in it?

Prayer: Remind me always, Lord, my place at your table is by your gracious invitation and not my worthiness.

Prepared for Trouble[142]

When they had sung a hymn, they went out to the Mount of Olives.

Then Jesus said to them, "All of you will be made to stumble because of me tonight, for it is written, 'I will strike the shepherd, and the sheep of the flock will be scattered.' But after I am raised up, I will go before you into Galilee."

Simon Peter said to him, "Lord, where are you going?"

Jesus answered, "Where I am going, you can't follow now, but you will follow afterwards. Simon, Simon, Satan asked to have you, to sift you as wheat; I prayed for you, that your faith wouldn't fail. After you have turned again, encourage the others."

Peter answered him, "Even if all will be made to stumble because of you, I will

---

Jesus saw what was coming and knew his disciples were far from ready. He told them to arm themselves and yet said two swords was enough for all of them: the battles they would soon face could never be won with weapons. How prepared are you for the crises of life? Do you think those who are heavily armed feel safer in today's world?

Prayer: Give me strength, Lord, to follow you no matter what.

---

[141] Matthew 26:26-29; Mark 14:22-25; Luke 22:15-20

[142] Matthew 26:30-35; Mark 14:26-31; Luke 22:31-38; John 13:36-38

never do so."

Jesus said to him, "Tonight, before the rooster crows, you will deny me three times."

Peter said to him, "Even if I must die with you, I will not deny you." All of the disciples said the same.

He said to them, "When I sent you out without purse, and wallet, and shoes, did you lack anything?"

They said, "Nothing."

Then he said to them, "But now, whoever has a purse, let him take it, and likewise a wallet. Whoever has none, let him sell his cloak, and buy a sword. For I tell you that this which is written must still be fulfilled in me: 'He was counted with transgressors.' For that which concerns me has an end."

They said, "Lord, we have two swords."

He said to them, "That is enough."

Jesus is the Way[143]

Jesus said, "Don't let your hearts be troubled. Believe in God. Believe also in me. In my Father's house are many homes. If it weren't so, I would have told you. I am going to prepare a place for you. If I go and prepare a place for you, I will come again, and will receive you to myself; that where I am, you may be there also. You know where I go, and you know the way."

Thomas said to him, "Lord, we don't know where you are going. How can we know the way?"

Jesus said to him, "I am the way, the truth, and the life. No one comes to the Father, except through me. If you had known me, you would have known my Father also. From now on, you know him, and have seen him."

Philip said to him, "Lord, show us the Father, and that will be enough for us."

Jesus said to him, "Have I been with you such a long time, and do you not know me, Philip? He who has seen me has seen the Father. How do

---

It is hard to imagine any more outlandish claim than saying you are the only way to God and whoever has seen you has seen God. Such claims indicate a person who is certifiably crazy, a world-class liar, or someone unlike anyone else who ever lived. Are there other options? Is the choice clear to you?

Prayer: Forgive me, Lord, for thinking I could ignore the claims you made.

---

[143] John 14:1-14

you say, 'Show us the Father?' Don't you believe that I am in the Father, and the Father in me? The words that I tell you, I speak not from myself; but the Father who lives in me does his works. Believe me that I am in the Father, and the Father in me; or else believe me for the works I do. Whoever believes in me will do the works I do, and greater works than these, because I am going to my Father. Whatever you ask in my name, I will do that the Father may be glorified in the Son. If you will ask anything in my name, I will do it.

The Promise of the Holy Spirit[144]

If you love me, keep my commandments. I will pray to the Father, and he will give you another Counselor to be with you forever, the Spirit of truth, whom the world can't receive because it doesn't see him or know him. You do know him, for he lives with you, and will be in you. I will not leave you as orphans; I will come to you. Yet a little while, and the world will see me no more; but you will see me. Because I live, you will live also. In that day you will know that I am in my Father, and you are in me, and I am in you. Those who have my commandments and keep them are the ones who love me, and will be loved by my Father, and I will love them and will reveal myself to them."

There is a clear sequence here: if we love Jesus, we will faithfully live out his commands; if we live faithfully, we will experience the presence of Jesus through the indwelling of the Holy Spirit. Does this sequence connect with your spiritual journey? Where are you on the journey now and what might the next step be?

Prayer: Thank you, Lord, for the journey and your presence on it with me all the way.

Judas (not Iscariot) said to him, "Lord, what has happened that you are about to reveal yourself to us, and not to the world?"

Jesus answered him, "Those who love me will keep my word. My Father will love them, and we will come to them, and make our home with them. Those who don't love me don't keep my words. The word you hear isn't mine: it is the word of the Father who sent me. I have said these things to you while still with you, but the Counselor, the Holy Spirit, whom the Father will send in my name, will teach you all things, and will remind you of all that I said to you.

Peace I leave with you. My peace I give you, not as the world gives. Don't let your heart be troubled or fearful. I told you, 'I go away, and I

---

[144] John 14:15-31

come to you.' If you loved me, you would have rejoiced, because I said 'I am going to my Father;' for the Father is greater than I. I have told you before it happens, so when it happens, you may believe. I will not speak much more with you, for the prince of the world comes and has no part of me. For the world to know I love the Father, I do what the Father tells me. Arise, let us go from here.

Dwell in Me[145]

"I am the true vine, and my Father is the farmer. Every branch in me that doesn't bear fruit, he takes away. Every branch that bears fruit, he prunes that it may bear more fruit. You are already pruned because of the word I have spoken to you. Dwell in me, and I in you. As the branch can't bear fruit by itself, unless it dwells in the vine, so neither can you, unless you dwell in me. I am the vine; you are the branches. If you dwell in me, and I in you, you will bear much fruit; apart from me you can do nothing. If you don't dwell in me, you will be cut off like a branch that withers; these are good only to gather, throw into the fire, and burn. If you dwell in me, and my words dwell in you, you will ask whatever you desire, and it will be done for you.

The word "dwell" appears repeatedly in this passage, and is sometimes translated as "abide," "remain," or "live in." This intimate connection with Jesus allows us to be fruitful even when the world stands in opposition to us. What does this idea of "dwell" look like in your life? Would you say your connection with Jesus is becoming more intimate or that you are drifting apart?

Prayer: Draw me close to you, Lord, that I might increasingly live in your love and extend your love to others.

"In this is my Father glorified, that you bear much fruit; and so you will be my disciples. Even as the Father has loved me, I also have loved you. Dwell in my love. If you keep my commandments, you will dwell in my love; even as I have kept my Father's commandments and dwell in his love. I have spoken these things to you that my joy may dwell in you, and that your joy may be made full.

"This is my commandment, that you love one another even as I have loved you. Greater love has no one than this, to lay down your life for your friends. You are my friends, if you do what I tell you. No longer do I call you servants, for the servant doesn't know what the master does. I have called you friends because everything I heard from my Father I have

---

[145] John 15:1-25

made known to you. You didn't choose me, but I chose you, and appointed you, that you should go and bear fruit, and that your fruit should last; whatever you ask of the Father in my name, he will give you.

"I tell you to love one another. If the world hates you, know that it hated me before it hated you. If you were of the world, the world would love you as its own. You are not of the world because I chose you out of the world. Therefore the world hates you. Remember the word I said to you: 'A servant is not greater than his lord.' If they persecuted me, they will also persecute you. If they kept my word, they would keep yours also. But all these things they will do to you for my name's sake, because they don't know him who sent me. If I had not come and spoken to them, they wouldn't have been guilty; but now they have no excuse for their sin. Whoever hates me, hates my Father also. If I hadn't done among them the works no one else did, they wouldn't have been guilty. But now have they seen and hated both me and my Father. This fulfilled what was written in their law, 'They hated me without a cause.'

The Work of the Holy Spirit[146]

"When the Counselor I will send to you from the Father, the Spirit of truth, has come, he will testify about me. You will also testify, because you have been with me from the beginning.

"These things I have told you, so you wouldn't stumble. You will be put out of the synagogues. Yes, the time is coming when whoever kills you will see it as a service to God. They will do these things because they have known neither the Father nor me. I have told you these things, so when the time comes, you'll remember I told you about them. I didn't tell you these things earlier, because I was with you. Now I am going to him who sent me, and none of you asks me, 'Where are you going?' But because I have told you these things, sorrow has filled your heart. I tell you the truth: it is to your advantage I go away, for if I don't go away, the Counselor won't come to you. But if I go, I

More than simply a comforting sense of God's presence, the Holy Spirit plays an active role in the lives of believers, bestowing spiritual gifts, developing spiritual fruit, guiding and directing. Can you think of times when you have sensed the Holy Spirit's presence and power in your life? Can you tell the difference between your own ideas and those coming from the Holy Spirit?

Prayer: Fill me with your Spirit, Lord, that I might make a difference in the lives of others.

[146] John 15:26-16:15

will send him to you. When he has come, he will convict the world about sin, about righteousness, and about judgment; about sin, because they don't believe in me; about righteousness, because I am going to my Father, and you won't see me anymore; about judgment, because the prince of this world has been judged.

"I have yet many things to tell you, but you can't bear them now. However when the Spirit of truth has come, he will guide you into all truth, for he will not speak from himself; whatever he hears, he will speak. He will declare to you things that are coming. He will glorify me, for he will take from what is mine, and will declare it to you. Everything the Father has is mine; that is why I said he takes of mine, and will declare it to you. A little while, and you will not see me. Again a little while, and you will see me."

Sorrow Turned to Joy[147]

Some of his disciples said to one another, "What does he mean when he says, 'A little while, and you won't see me, and again a little while, and you will see me;' and, 'Because I go to the Father'? We don't know what he is saying."

Jesus understood what they wanted to ask him, and said to them, "Do you wonder what this means? You will weep and lament, but the world will rejoice; you will be sorrowful, but your sorrow will be turned into joy. A woman, when she gives birth, suffers because her time has come. When she has delivered the child, she doesn't remember the anguish anymore because of her joy that a baby is born. You now suffer, but I will see you again, and your heart will rejoice, and no one will take your joy away from you.

The disciples had listened to Jesus for three years, but still struggled to understand what he meant by his death and resurrection. This was not the triumphant Messiah they had been told to expect. Have you been surprised by God answering a prayer in a way you hadn't expected? How can these surprises impact the way you pray?

Prayer: Thank you, Lord, for being surprised when sorrow turns to joy.

"In that day you will ask me no questions. Whatever you ask of the Father in my name, he will give you. Until now, you have asked nothing in my name. Ask, and you will receive, that your joy may be made full. I have spoken these things to you in figures of speech. But the time is coming when I will no more speak to

147 John 16:16-33

you in figures of speech, but will tell you plainly about the Father. In that day you will ask in my name; I don't say I will pray to the Father for you, for the Father himself loves you, because you have loved me, and have believed that I came from God. I came from the Father, and have come into the world. Again, I leave the world, and go to the Father."

His disciples said to him, "Now you speak plainly without figures of speech. Now we know that you know all things, and don't need for anyone to question you. By this we believe you came from God."

Jesus answered them, "Do you now believe? The time has come that you will be scattered, each of you to your own place, and you will abandon me. Yet I am not alone, because the Father is with me. I have told you these things, that in me you may have peace. In the world you have oppression; but cheer up! I have overcome the world."

Praying for Us[148]

Jesus said these things, and lifting up his eyes to heaven, said, "Father, the time has come. Glorify your Son, that your Son may also glorify you; even as you gave him authority over all flesh, he will give eternal life to all whom you have given him. This is eternal life, that they should know you, the only true God, and the one you sent, Jesus Christ. I glorified you on the earth, and accomplished the work you gave me to do. Now, Father, glorify me with your own self, the glory I had with you before the world existed. I revealed your name to the people you gave me out of the world. They were yours, and you gave them to me. They have kept your word. Now they know all things you gave me are from you; the words you gave me I gave them, and they received them; they know I came from you, and they have believed you sent me. I pray for them. I don't pray for the world, but for those whom you gave me, for they are yours. All things that are mine are yours, and yours are mine, and I am glorified in them. I am no more in the world; I am coming to you, but they are in the world. Holy Father, keep them through your name, that they may be one, even as we are one. While I was with them, I kept them in your name. None of them is lost, except the son of destruction, that the Scripture might be fulfilled. Now I come to you. I say these things in the world that they may have my joy made full in themselves. I have given them your word. The world hated them,

[148] John 17:1-26

because they are not of the world, even as I am not of the world. I pray not that you would take them from the world, but that you would keep them from the evil one. They are not of the world even as I am not of the world. Sanctify them in your truth. Your word is truth. As you sent me into the world, even so I have sent them into the world. For their sakes I sanctify myself, that they also may be sanctified in truth. Not for these only do I pray, but for those also who believe in me through their word, that they may all be one, even as you, Father, are in me, and I in you. May they also be one in us; that the world will believe you sent me. The glory you gave me, I gave them that they may be one, even as we are one; I in them, and you in me, whole and complete, that the world may know you sent me, and loved them, even as you loved me. Father, I want them also to be with me where I am, that they may see my glory, which you have given me, for you loved me before the foundation of the world. Righteous Father, the world hasn't known you, but I knew you, and they knew you sent me. I made known to them your name, and will make it known, that the love with which you loved me may be in them, and I in them."

It is common to think eternal life refers to what happens after we die, but Jesus says eternal life is to know him, and God through him. This eternal life is not about living forever in heaven, but having here and now a unique quality of life, the good life, abundant life. How much is your faith centered on going to heaven? Is following Jesus its own reward?

Prayer: What a privilege and blessing, Lord, to connect with you now and look forward to an amazing future!

Chapter 9: The Crucifixion

Praying in Gethsemane[149]

They came to a place named Gethsemane. He said to his disciples, "Sit here, while I pray." He took with him Peter, James, and John, and began to be greatly troubled and distressed. He said to them, "My soul is exceedingly sorrowful, even to death. Stay here, and watch."

*In the Lord's Prayer, Jesus **told** us how to pray; in Gethsemane, Jesus **showed** us how to pray. He told God what he wanted ("If possible, let me avoid this cup of suffering"), and then he subordinated his desire to God's will ("Not my will but yours be done"). Are your prayers like this or do you have trouble getting beyond telling God what you want?*

Prayer: Remind me what you prayed in Gethsemane, Lord, whenever I start putting my desires ahead of your will.

He went forward a little, and fell on the ground, and prayed that, if it were possible, the hour might pass away from him. He said, "Abba, Father, all things are possible to you. Please remove this cup from me. However, not my will, but yours, be done."

He came and found them sleeping, and said to Peter, "Are you sleeping? Couldn't you watch one hour? Watch and pray, that you not enter into temptation. The spirit indeed is willing, but the flesh is weak."

Again he went away, and prayed, saying the same words. Again he returned, and found them sleeping, for their eyes were very heavy, and they didn't know what to answer him. He came the third time, and said to them, "You've slept now, and taken your rest. It is enough. The hour has come. The Son of Man is betrayed into the hands of sinners. Get up and get ready; he who betrays me is at hand."

---

[149] Matthew 26:36-46; Mark 14:32-42; Luke 22:39-46; John 18:1

Betrayed by a Kiss[150]

While he was still speaking, Judas came, and with him a great crowd with swords and clubs, from the chief priest and elders of the people. He had given them a sign: "Whoever I kiss is the one. Seize him." Then he went to Jesus, and said, "Hello, Rabbi!" and kissed him.

Jesus said to him, "Friend, why are you here?" Then they came and laid hands on Jesus, and took him. One of those with Jesus drew his sword, and struck the servant of the high priest, cutting off his ear. Jesus said to him, "Put your sword back into its place, for all those who take the sword will die by the sword. Or do you think I couldn't ask my Father, and he would send me more than twelve legions of angels? How then would the Scriptures be fulfilled that it must be so?"

Jesus said to the crowd, "Have you come out as if I were a robber, with swords and clubs to seize me? I sat daily in the temple teaching, and you didn't arrest me. But all this has happened, that the Scriptures of the prophets might be fulfilled."

Then all the disciples left him, and fled.

Those who came to arrest Jesus needed someone to point him out. They had never met him, never heard him speak, never seen his miracles, and yet they were ready to arrest him and kill him. People today still find it easy to condemn those they've never met. What shapes your opinion of people? Are you influenced by media or by the opinions of friends? Is there anyone you can trust to give you an unbiased opinion?

Prayer: Confront me, Lord, when I allow my view of someone I have never met to be shaped by what I have heard from others.

Peter's Denial[151]

The detachment, the commanding officer, and the officer of the Jews, seized Jesus and bound him, and led him first to Annas, father-in-law to Caiaphas, the high priest that year who had advised the Jews it was expedient that one man should perish for the people. Simon Peter followed Jesus, as did another disciple. The other disciple was known to the high priest, and entered in with Jesus to the court of the high priest, but Peter stood at the door outside until the other disciple went out and spoke to the doorkeeper, and brought in Peter. Then the maid who kept the door said to Peter, "You were also with the Nazarene, Jesus. Are you

150 Matthew 26:47-56; Mark 14:43-52; Luke 22:47-53; John 18:2-12
151 Matthew 26:69-75; Mark 14:66-72; Luke 22:54-62; John 18:25-27

one of his disciples?"

He denied it, saying, "I'm not. I don't know or understand what you say."

The servants and the officers were standing there, warming themselves from a fire of coals, for it was cold. Peter was with them, standing and warming himself. The maid saw him, and began again to tell those who stood by, "This is one of them." But he again denied it, saying, "Woman, I don't know him."

After about an hour, those who stood by said to Peter, "You truly are one of them, for you are a Galilean, and your speech shows it." But he began to curse, and to swear, "I don't know this man of whom you speak!"

During the Last Supper, Peter was confident he would never deny Jesus, but only a few hours later he denied him three times. Have you ever over-estimated your ability to resist temptation or show courage in the face of conflict? What effect did your actions (or lack of action) have on your self-image and self-confidence?

Prayer: Forgive me, Lord, for thinking I can handle life's challenges in my own strength.

While he was still speaking, a rooster crowed. The Lord turned, and looked at Peter. Then Peter remembered the Lord's word, how he said to him, "Before the rooster crows you will deny me three times." He went out, and wept bitterly.

The Sanhedrin Trial[152]

The men who held Jesus mocked him and beat him. Having blindfolded him, they struck him on the face and told him, "Prophesy! Who is the one who struck you?" They spoke many other things against him, insulting him.

As soon as it was day, the assembly of the elders was gathered together, both chief priests and scribes, and they led him away into their council. The chief priests and the whole council sought witnesses against Jesus to put him to death, and found none. Many gave false testimony against him, and their statements didn't agree. Some stood up, and said, "We heard him say, 'I will destroy this temple that is made with hands, and in three days I will build another made without hands.'" Even so, their testimony did not agree.

The high priest stood up in the middle, and asked Jesus, "Have you

[152] Matthew 26:57-68; Mark 14:53-65; Luke 22:63-71; John 18:12-24

no answer to what they say against you?" But he stayed quiet, and answered nothing.

They said to him, "If you are the Christ, tell us."

He said to them, "If I tell you, you won't believe, and if I ask, you won't answer me or let me go. Soon the Son of Man will be seated at the right hand of the power of God."

They all said, "Are you then the Son of God?"

He said to them, "You say it, because I am."

They said, "Why do we need any more witnesses? We have heard this blasphemy from his own mouth!"

Again the high priest asked him, "Are you the Christ, the Son of the Blessed?"

Jesus said, "I am. You will see the Son of Man sitting at the right hand of Power, and coming with the clouds of the sky."

The high priest tore his clothes, and said, "What further need is there for witnesses? You've heard the blasphemy! What do you think?" They all said he was worthy of death. Some began to spit on him, and cover his face, and beat him with fists, and say, "Prophesy!" The officers struck him with the palms of their hands.

Perjured testimony is rarely convincing because it is so often inconsistent and contradictory. Ultimately Jesus was convicted by his own words. Claiming to be the Son of God demanded a response: they could either bow down and acknowledge him as their true king or condemn him for blasphemy. The religious leaders chose the latter. How do you respond to Jesus? Do you acknowledge him as Lord and live accordingly?

Prayer: Help me see you as you are, Lord, and respond to you with integrity.

The Death of Judas[153]

When Judas saw Jesus condemned, he felt remorse for betraying him, and brought back the thirty pieces of silver to the chief priests and elders, saying, "I have sinned by betraying innocent blood."

But they said, "What is that to us? You see to it."

He threw down the pieces of silver in the sanctuary, and departed. He went away and hanged himself. The chief priests took the pieces of silver, and said, "It's not lawful to put it into the treasury, since it is the price of blood." They took counsel, and bought the potter's field for the

[153] Matthew 27:3-10

Though a number of explanations have been suggested for Judas' betrayal, none is particularly compelling. We may never be sure why he did it, but we know he regretted it; he even tried to return the money, but for him there was no do-over. Have you ever made a decision you later came to regret? What factors led to your decision?

Prayer: Help me be discerning, Lord, lest I make decisions I later regret.

burial of strangers. That field is called "The Field of Blood" to this day. This fulfilled what was spoken through Jeremiah the prophet:

"They took the thirty pieces of silver,
the price of him upon whom a price had been set,
whom some of the children of Israel priced,
and they gave them for the potter's field,
as the Lord commanded me."

Herod and Pilate[154]

When morning had come, all the chief priests and the elders of the people took counsel against Jesus to put him to death; they bound him, led him away, and delivered him to Pontius Pilate, the governor.

Pilate went out to the crowd, and said, "What accusation do you bring against this man?"

They answered him, "If this man weren't an evildoer, we wouldn't have delivered him up to you."

Pilate said, "Take him yourselves, and judge him according to your law."

The Jews replied, "It is not lawful for us to crucify anyone. We found this man perverting the nation, forbidding paying taxes to Caesar, and saying that he himself is Christ, a king."

Pilate entered again into the Praetorium, called Jesus, and said to him, "Are you the king of the Jews?"

Jesus answered, "Do you say this yourself, or did others tell you about me?"

Pilate answered, "I'm not a Jew, am I? Your own nation and the chief priests delivered you to me. What have you done?"

Jesus answered, "My kingdom is not of this world. If my kingdom were of this world, then my servants would fight, that I wouldn't be delivered to the Jews. But my kingdom is not from here."

Pilate said to him, "Are you a king then?"

Jesus answered, "You say that I am a king. For this reason I have been

---

[154] Matthew 27:1-2,11-14; Mark 15:1-5; Luke 23:1-12; John 18:28-38

born, and for this reason I have come into the world, that I should testify to the truth. Everyone who is of the truth listens to my voice."

Pilate said to him, "What is truth?"

When he had said this, he went out again to the Jews, and said to them, "I find no basis for a charge against him." Pilate asked if Jesus was a Galilean. When he found out he was, he sent him to Herod, who was in Jerusalem at the time.

When Herod saw Jesus, he was very happy because he had wanted to see him for a long time; he had heard many things, and hoped to see him do some miracle. He questioned him with many words, but Jesus gave no answers. The chief priests and the scribes stood nearby, vehemently accusing him. Herod with his soldiers humiliated him and mocked him, and then sent him back to Pilate. Herod and Pilate, who had been enemies, became friends with each other that day.

Herod and Pilate ruled Galilee and Judea, answering to no one except the emperor in Rome. Both were curious, but neither took Jesus seriously. Do you know people who think little of Jesus? How do you respond to those who don't take him seriously?

Prayer: When I am in a position to exercise power, Lord, help me keep my heart tender and open to you.

The Humiliated King[155]

Pilate's soldiers stripped Jesus, and put a scarlet robe on him. They braided a crown of thorns and put it on his head, and a reed in his right hand; and they knelt down before him, and mocked him, saying, "Hail, King of the Jews!" They spit on him, and took the reed and struck him on the head. They took him out, wearing the crown of thorns and the purple garment, and Pilate said to the crowd, "Behold, the man!"

When the chief priests and officers saw him, they shouted, "Crucify! Crucify!"

Pilate said to them, "Take him yourselves, and crucify him. I find no basis for a charge against him."

The Jews answered him, "We have a law, and by our law he ought to die, because he made himself the Son of God."

When Pilate heard this, he was more afraid. He entered into the Praetorium again, and said to Jesus, "Where are you from?" But Jesus gave him no answer. Pilate therefore said to him, "Aren't you speaking to

---

155 Matthew 27:24-31; Mark 15:15-20; Luke 23:24-25; John 19:1-16

me? Don't you know that I have power to release you or to crucify you?"

Jesus answered, "You would have no power at all against me, unless it were given to you from above. Therefore he who delivered me to you has greater sin."

At this, Pilate was seeking to release him, but the Jews cried out, saying, "If you release this man, you aren't Caesar's friend! Everyone who makes himself a king speaks against Caesar!"

When Pilate therefore heard these words, he brought Jesus out, and sat down on the judgment seat at a place called "The Pavement", but in Hebrew, "Gabbatha." Now it was the Preparation Day of the Passover, at about the sixth hour. He said to the Jews, "Behold, your king!"

Pilate didn't believer Jesus was the Christ, but still he didn't want to be responsible for the death of what he considered an extraordinary man. His power was limited, though, by fear the Jews would report him to Rome as weak if he didn't have Jesus crucified. Have you ever felt pressured into a decision you didn't want to make? What was the nature of the fear you felt?

Prayer: Give me the courage I need, Lord, when I'm feeling pressure to do something I know isn't right.

They cried out, "Away with him! Away with him! Crucify him!"

Pilate said to them, "Shall I crucify your king?"

The chief priests answered, "We have no king but Caesar!"

The Crowd Prevails[156]

Pilate said to them, "You brought this man to me as one who perverts the people. I have examined him before you, and found no basis for a charge against this man concerning those things of which you accuse him. Neither has Herod, for I sent you to him. Nothing worthy of death has been done by him. I will therefore flog him and release him."

The governor's custom was to release a prisoner at Passover to please the people. He said to the crowd, "Who do you want me to release to you? Barabbas or Jesus, who is called Christ?" Barabbas was a notorious murderer, and Pilate knew it was because of envy the Jewish leaders had arrested Jesus.

While he was sitting on the judgment seat, his wife sent to him, saying, "Have nothing to do with that righteous man; I have suffered many things today in a dream because of him."

---

[156] Matthew 27:15-23; Mark 15:6-14; Luke 23:13-23; John 18:39-40

The chief priests and elders persuaded the crowd to ask for Barabbas, and crucify Jesus. The governor asked again, "So which of the two do you want me to release to you?" They cried out together, "Away with this man! Give us Barabbas!"

Then Pilate, wanting to release Jesus, spoke to them again, but they shouted, "Crucify him! Crucify him!"

He said to them a third time, "Why? What evil has this man done? I have found no crime in him. I will therefore flog him and release him." But they demanded with loud voices he be crucified, and their voices prevailed.

When Pilate saw nothing was being gained, but a disturbance was growing, he took water, and washed his hands before the crowd, saying, "I am innocent of the blood of this righteous person. You see to it."

All the people answered, "May his blood be on us, and on our children!"

Pilate released Barabbas, and had Jesus flogged and delivered to be crucified.

The cruelty of those who mocked and abused Jesus knew no bounds. Some of the things humans do to one another are almost unthinkable, and yet such cruelty is all too common in human history. Have you ever been treated cruelly? Have you ever been part of a group treating others badly? Why did you go along with what the others did?

Prayer: Help me remember how you suffered, Lord, when I see others being bullied and abused.

The Way of the Cross[157]

When they led him away, they grabbed a bystander, Simon of Cyrene, and laid on him the cross, to carry it for Jesus. A great crowd followed, including women who mourned and lamented him. Jesus, turning to them, said, "Daughters of Jerusalem, don't weep for me, but weep for yourselves and for your children. For behold, the days are coming in which they will say, 'Blessed are the barren, the wombs that never bore, and the breasts that never nursed.' Then they will begin to tell the mountains, 'Fall on us!' and tell the hills, 'Cover us.' For if they do these things when the tree is green, what will be done when it is dried up?"

He went out, bearing his cross, to the place called "The Place of a Skull", which is called in Hebrew, "Golgotha", where they crucified him, and two others, with Jesus in the middle.

Jesus said, "Father, forgive them, for they don't know what they are

157 Matthew 27:31-37; Mark 15:20-26; Luke 23:26-34; John 19:17-27

doing."

Pilate wrote a sign, and put it on the cross, saying, "JESUS OF NAZARETH, THE KING OF THE JEWS." Many of the Jews read this title, for the place where Jesus was crucified was near the city; it was written in Hebrew, Latin, and Greek. The chief priests of the Jews said to Pilate, "Don't write, 'The King of the Jews,' but, 'he said, I am King of the Jews.'"

Pilate answered, "What I have written, I have written."

The enormity of the crucifixion is only matched by the significance of Jesus saying, "Father, forgive them for they don't know what they are doing." The way in which Jesus puts into practice his command to love your enemies is breathtaking. Could you ever imagine doing something like this? What other examples of such love and forgiveness have you encountered?

Prayer: In dealing with those who have abused me, Lord, give me the grace I need to forgive them and so avoid an abyss of hatred and vengeance.

Then the soldiers, when they had crucified Jesus, took his garments and made four parts, to every soldier a part; and also the cloak. Now the cloak was without seam, woven from the top throughout. Then they said to one another, "Let's not tear it, but cast lots for it to decide whose it will be." This fulfilled the Scripture which says,

"They parted my garments among them.
For my cloak they cast lots."

The soldiers did these things, while his mother and his mother's sister, Mary the wife of Clopas, and Mary Magdalen were standing by the cross. When Jesus saw his mother, and John, the disciple whom he loved, standing there, he said to his mother, "Woman, behold your son!" Then he said to John, "Behold your mother!" From that hour, the disciple took her to his own home.

Thieves on the Cross[158]

There were two robbers crucified with him, one on his right hand and one on the left. Those who passed by mocked him, wagging their heads, and saying, "You who would destroy the temple, and build it in three days, save yourself! If you are the Son of God, come down from the cross!"

Likewise the chief priests mocking with the scribes, Pharisees and elders, said, "He saved others, but he can't save himself. If he is the King of Israel, let him come down from the cross now and we'll believe in him.

---

158 Matthew 27:38-44; Mark 15:27-32; Luke 23:35-43;

He trusts in God and says he is the Son of God: let God deliver him!"

One of the criminals on the cross insulted him, saying, "If you are the Christ, save yourself and us!"

But the other rebuked him, saying, "Don't you even fear God, seeing you are under the same condemnation? For us it is justice, punishment for what we've done, but this man has done nothing wrong." He said to Jesus, "Lord, remember me when you come into your kingdom."

Jesus said to him, "I tell you, today you will be with me in Paradise."

Crucifixion was a gruesome form of punishment used to keep in line slaves and rebels like those crucified with Jesus. One of the criminals spoke with anger and bitterness as expected; the other showed a humble heart, tender toward God. Have you known people who were like these two criminals? How would you respond to each one?

Prayer: Help me remember that no two people are alike, Lord, and outward appearances can often be deceiving.

The Death of Jesus[159]

Now from the sixth hour there was darkness over all the land until the ninth hour. About the ninth hour Jesus cried out with a loud voice, "Eli, Eli, lima sabachthani?" That is, "My God, my God, why have you forsaken me?"

Some who stood there, when they heard it, said, "This man is calling Elijah."

One of them ran, and took a sponge, and filled it with vinegar, and put it on a reed, and gave him a drink. The rest said, "Let him be. Let's see whether Elijah comes to save him."

Jesus cried again with a loud voice, and yielded up his spirit. The veil of the temple was torn in two from the top to the bottom. The earth quaked and rocks were split. Tombs were opened, and many bodies of saints who had died were raised; coming out of the tombs after his resurrection, they entered into the holy city and appeared to many. The centurion and those who were with him watching

---

The end of Jesus' life was accompanied by signs and wonders, some of which are hard to understand. The Roman officer watching all of this came to believe Jesus was indeed the Son of God as he had claimed. What conclusions have you reached concerning Jesus? What about the death (or life) of Jesus have you found most compelling?

Prayer: Keep the mystery and the majesty of the cross, Lord, ever before me.

---

159 Matthew 27:45-56; Mark 15:33-41; Luke 23:44-49; John 19:28-30

Jesus feared greatly when they saw the earthquake and the things that were done. They said, "Truly this was the Son of God."

There were also women watching from afar, including Mary Magdalene, and Mary, the mother of Joses, who followed Jesus and served him when he was in Galilee, along with many other women who came up with him to Jerusalem.

The Burial of Jesus[160]

The Jews, because it was the Preparation Day, and not wanting the bodies to remain on the cross on the Passover Sabbath, asked Pilate that their legs might be broken, and the bodies taken away. The soldiers came, and broke the legs of the first, and of the other who was crucified with him, but when they came to Jesus, and saw that he was already dead, they didn't break his legs. However one of the soldiers pierced his side with a spear, and immediately blood and water came out. One who saw this has testified, and his testimony is true; he tells the truth for you to believe. These things happened to fulfill the Scripture, "A bone of him will not be broken," and another, "They will look on him whom they pierced."

At dusk, Joseph of Arimathaea, a prominent council member who himself was looking for God's kingdom, went boldly to Pilate, and asked for Jesus' body. Pilate marveled that he was already dead; summoning the centurion, he asked him whether he had been dead long. When he found out from the centurion, he granted the body to Joseph, who bought a linen cloth, and taking him down, wound him in the linen cloth, and laid him in a tomb cut out of a rock. He rolled a stone against the door of the tomb. Mary Magdalene and Mary, the mother of Joses, saw where he was laid.

The next day, the chief priests and Pharisees came to Pilate, saying, "Sir, we remember what that deceiver said while he was still alive: 'After three days I will rise again.' Command that the tomb be made secure until the third day, lest his disciples come at night and steal him away, and tell the people, 'He is risen from the dead;' and the last deception will be worse than the first."

---

[160] Matthew 27:57-66; Mark 15:42-47; Luke 23:50-56; John 19:31-42

Pilate said to them, "You have a guard. Go, make it as secure as you can." They went with the guard and made the tomb secure, sealing the stone.

The religious leaders who brought about the death of Jesus wanted to make sure of three things: 1) that he was dead; 2) that he was buried; and 3) that no one tampered with his tomb. This was to be the exclamation point bringing his life to an end. How would your life be different if indeed this had been the end of the story? Would you still cling to the memory of Jesus and the things he said and did?

Prayer: Thank you, Lord, this isn't the end of the story, but in many ways only the beginning.

Chapter 10: The Resurrection

Sunday Morning[161]

When the Sabbath was over, Mary Magdalene, and Mary the mother of Joses, bought spices, that they might come and anoint Jesus. The next morning, they came to the tomb at sunrise. They said to each other, "Who will roll away the stone from the door of the tomb for us?" because it was very big.

The grief of Friday and Saturday turned into the confusion of Sunday. The women went early to anoint the body, wondering who would roll back the stone. The tomb was empty except for discarded grave clothes. One disciple saw and believed; the others didn't know what to think. If you had been there, what would you have thought?

Prayer: Thank you for evidence of the resurrection, Lord, and for faith that comes before the evidence is all in.

There was a great earthquake as an angel of the Lord descended from the heavens, and rolled away the stone from the door, and sat on it. His appearance was like lightning, and his clothing white as snow. For fear of him, the guards shook, and became like dead men.

Entering into the tomb, the women were amazed to see a young man dressed in a white robe, sitting on the right side. He said to them, "Don't be amazed. You seek Jesus, the Nazarene, who was crucified. He is not here, for he has risen, just like he said. See the place where they laid him! Go quickly and tell his disciples and Peter. He goes before you into Galilee. There you will see him, as he said to you."

They departed quickly from the tomb with fear and great joy, and ran to bring his disciples word.

Mary ran to Simon Peter and John, saying to them, "They have taken away the Lord out of the tomb, and we don't know where they have laid him!"

Peter and John ran together to the tomb. John outran Peter, and came to the tomb first. Stooping and looking in, he saw the linen cloths

---

161 Matthew 28:1-8; Mark 16:1-8; Luke 24:1-12; John 20:1-13

lying there, yet he didn't enter. Then Peter came and entered into the tomb. He saw the linen cloths lying there, and the cloth that had been on his head, not lying with the linen cloths, but rolled up in a place by itself. Then John also entered; he saw and believed, though as yet they didn't know the Scripture that he must rise from the dead. So the disciples went away again to their homes.

Jesus Appears to Mary[162]

Mary was standing outside the tomb weeping. As she wept, she stooped and looked into the tomb and saw two angels in white sitting, one at the head, and one at the feet, where the body of Jesus had been. They asked her, "Woman, why are you weeping?"

She said to them, "They have taken away my Lord, and I don't know where they have laid him." As she said this, she turned and saw Jesus standing there, but didn't know it was him.

Jesus said to her, "Woman, why are you weeping? Who are you looking for?"

Supposing him to be the gardener, she said to him, "Sir, if you have carried him away, tell me where you have laid him, and I will go get him."

Jesus said to her, "Mary."

She went to him and said, "Rabboni!" which is to say, "Teacher!"

Jesus said to her, "Don't hold on to me, for I haven't yet ascended to my Father, but go to the others, and tell them I am ascending to my Father and your Father, to my God and your God."

The resurrected Jesus wasn't recognizable at first. Only when Jesus called her by name did Mary know who he was. What would it mean for Jesus to call you by name today? Can there be an intimate connection even if there is no audible voice?

Prayer: Thank you for the still, small voice, Lord, speaking my name and telling me of your love.

Mary went to the disciples and told them she had seen the Lord, and he had said these things to her.

While this was happening, the guards went into the city, and told the chief priests what had happened. When they had met with the elders for advice, they gave a large amount of silver to the soldiers, saying, "Tell everyone his disciples came by night and stole his body while you slept. If this comes to the governor's ears, we will exonerate you." The soldiers

162 Matthew 28:9-15; Mark 16:9-11; John 20:11-18

took the money and did as they were told. This saying was spread abroad among the Jews, and continues to this day.

The Road to Emmaus[163]

Two disciples were going that first day of the week to Emmaus, a village about seven miles from Jerusalem. They talked with each other about all of the things which had happened. While they talked and raised questions, Jesus himself came near and walked with them, but their eyes were kept from recognizing him. He said to them, "What are you talking about as you walk, and are so sad?"

One of them, Cleopas, answered, "Are you the only stranger in Jerusalem who doesn't know what happened here these days?"

He said to them, "What things?"

They said, "Things about Jesus, the Nazarene, who was a prophet mighty in deed and word before God and all the people. The chief priests and our rulers delivered him up to be condemned and crucified. We were hoping it was he who would redeem Israel.

Again, Jesus wasn't recognizable at first, but this time it was in the breaking of bread that the disciples saw him for who he was. Do you sense the presence of Jesus now in the breaking of bread or communion? Have you experienced a time when the scriptures have "burned within you" as you read them?

Prayer: Keep your word burning within me, Lord, as I sense your presence and feel your power.

It is now the third day since these things happened, and certain women of our company amazed us after going to the tomb early this morning. When they didn't find his body, they came saying they had seen a vision of angels, who told them he was alive. Some of us went to the tomb, and found it just like the women had said, but we didn't see him."

He said to them, "You are foolish, and slow of heart not to believe what the prophets spoke! Didn't the Christ have to suffer these things and enter into his glory?" Beginning from Moses and all the prophets, he explained to them in all the Scriptures the things concerning himself. They came near to the village where they were going, and he was prepared to continue his journey.

They urged him, "Stay with us, for the day is almost over."

He went in to stay with them. When he sat down at the table, he took the bread and gave thanks. Breaking it, he gave it to them. Their eyes

---

[163] Mark 16:12-13; Luke 24:13-35

were opened, and they recognized him, and then he vanished from their sight. They said to one another, "Weren't our hearts burning within us while he spoke to us along the road, and opened the Scriptures to us?" They rose up that very hour, returned to Jerusalem, and found the eleven gathered with others, saying, "The Lord is risen indeed, and has appeared to Simon!" They told what had happened along the way, and how Jesus was recognized by them in the breaking of the bread.

Resurrection Appearances[164]

As they talked, Jesus himself stood among them and said, "Peace be to you."

They were terrified, and supposed they had seen a spirit.

He said to them, "Why are you troubled? Why do doubts fill your hearts? See my hands and my feet, that it is truly me. Touch me and see, for a spirit doesn't have flesh and bones, as you see I have." When he had said this, he showed them his hands and his feet. While they still didn't believe and rejoice, but wondered, he said to them, "Do you have anything here to eat?"

They gave him a piece of broiled fish and some honeycomb. He took them, and ate in front of them before leaving.

Thomas, one of the twelve, wasn't with them when Jesus came. The other disciples said to him, "We have seen the Lord!"

But he said to them, "Unless I see the nail prints in his hands, and put my hand into his side, I will not believe."

Eight days later his disciples were inside, and Thomas was with them. The doors were locked, but Jesus came, stood in the middle, and said, "Peace be to you." Then he said to Thomas, "Touch my hands with your finger. Put your hand into my side. Don't be unbelieving, but believing."

Thomas answered him, "My Lord and my God!"

Jesus said to him, "Because you have seen me, you have believed. Blessed are

Thomas was a skeptic, unwilling to believe Jesus had been raised from the dead without clear and definite proof. Jesus gave him the proof he sought. Do you have trouble believing in the resurrection? What kind of evidence would it take to convince you?

Prayer: Thank you, Lord, for reacting to my skepticism with reassurances and not with condemnation.

164 Luke 24:36-43; John 20:19-29

those who have not seen, and yet have believed."

Back to Fishing[165]

A few days later, Peter, Thomas, Nathanael, the sons of Zebedee, and two others of his disciples were together. Peter said to them, "I'm going fishing."

They told him, "We're also coming with you." They went out on the sea of Tiberias in their boat, but that night they caught nothing. When day came and the boat returned, Jesus stood on the beach, though the disciples didn't know it was him. Jesus said to them, "Children, have you anything to eat?"

They answered him, "No."

He said, "Cast the net on the other side of the boat, and you will find some."

They did so, and now they weren't able to draw it in for the multitude of fish. John said to Peter, "It's the Lord!"

Though Jesus had already appeared twice to the disciples to convince them of the reality of his resurrection, they didn't know what to do next. Peter's idea was to go back to what he had been before he met Jesus and the others agreed. The results were disappointing until Jesus guided them. What are the default behaviors in your life, the things you do when you don't know what to do? How well do they work for you?

Prayer: Lead me to a new reality, Lord; break the habits that keep me going back to what I've always been.

When Peter heard it was the Lord, he wrapped his cloak around him (for he had disrobed), and threw himself into the sea. The other disciples came in the boat (for they were only about a hundred yards from shore), dragging the net full of fish. When they got out on the land, they saw a fire of coals there, and fish laid on it, and bread. Jesus said, "Bring some of the fish you just caught."

Peter went up, and drew the net to land, full of great fish, one hundred fifty-three in all; even though there were so many, the net wasn't torn.

Jesus said to them, "Come and eat breakfast." They knew it was Jesus, yet none of them dared ask, "Who are you?"

Peter's Restoration[166]

Jesus came and took the bread, and gave it to them, and the fish

---

165 John 21:1-12
166 John 21:12-25

likewise. This was the third time Jesus was revealed to his disciples after the resurrection.

When they had eaten their breakfast, Jesus said to Peter, "Simon, son of Jonah, do you love me more than these?"

He said to him, "Yes, Lord; you know I love you."

He said to him, "Feed my lambs." He said to him again a second time, "Simon, son of Jonah, do you love me?"

He said to him, "Yes, Lord; you know I love you."

He said to him, "Tend my sheep." He said to him the third time, "Simon, son of Jonah, do you love me?"

Peter was grieved because he asked him the third time, "Do you love me?" He said to him, "Lord, you know everything. You know I love you."

Jesus said to him, "Feed my sheep. I tell you, when you were young, you dressed yourself, and walked where you wanted to. But when you are old, you will stretch out your hands, and another will dress you, and carry you where you don't want to go."

Having denied Jesus three times before the crucifixion, Peter now was asked three times by Jesus if he loved him. This had to be excruciatingly difficult for Peter to experience, and yet it was filled with grace as well. Have you had a time of painful accountability in your life? Was grace extended to you in the midst of shame and guilt? Were you able to accept it?

Prayer: When faced with the enormity of my failures, Lord, help me accept the forgiveness and grace you offer.

Now he said this, signifying by what kind of death Peter would glorify God. After this, he said to him, "Follow me."

Then Peter, turning around, saw John following, and said to Jesus, "Lord, what about this man?"

Jesus said to him, "If I desire that he stay until I come, what is that to you? You follow me." This saying went out among the others that this disciple wouldn't die. Yet Jesus didn't say to him that he wouldn't die, but, "If I desire that he stay until I come, what is that to you?" This is the disciple who testifies about these things, and wrote these things. Know that his witness is true. There are also many other things Jesus did, which if they would all be written, even the world itself wouldn't have room enough for all of them.

Jesus' Last Words[167]

The eleven disciples went into Galilee, to the mountain where Jesus had sent them. When they saw him, they bowed down to him, but some doubted.

He said to them, "This is what I told you, while I was still with you, that all things which are written in the law of Moses, the prophets, and the psalms, concerning me must be fulfilled."

Then he opened their minds, that they might understand the Scriptures. He said to them, "Thus it is written, and thus it was necessary for the Christ to suffer and to rise from the dead the third day, and that repentance and remission of sins should be preached in his name to all the nations, beginning at Jerusalem.

"All authority has been given to me in heaven and on earth. Go, and make disciples of all nations, baptizing them in the name of the Father and of the Son and of the Holy Spirit, teaching them to observe all things that I commanded you. Behold, I am with you always, even to the end of the age."

"You are witnesses of these things. I send out the promise of my Father on you. But wait in the city of Jerusalem until you are clothed with power from on high."

He led them as far as Bethany, and lifted up his hands and blessed them. While he blessed them, he withdrew from them, and was carried up into heaven. They worshiped him, and returned to Jerusalem with great joy, and were continually in the temple, praising and blessing God.

The Great Commission given by Jesus was to go and make disciples, carrying on the kingdom work he began until such a time as he returned in the consummation of history. Have you taken the Great Commission as a personal call to action or do you see this as something only for "professionals" who are called to be ministers and missionaries? What is your next step?

Prayer: Thank you for the journey to which you have called me, Lord, and for being ready to lead me forward step by step.

---

[167] Matthew 28:16-20; Mark 16:9-20; Luke 24:44-53; John 20:30-31

The Next Step

Congratulations! You've finished the book. Or you've skipped ahead to this section. That's okay. In either case, it's time to decide what comes next. Here are some options for you to consider:

1. **You can learn more.** Reading this book may have raised as many questions for you as it answered. There are many outstanding scholars and authors dealing with any question you might have. Annotated reading lists are available on request.
2. **You can become a disciple.** You may have believed in Jesus before reading this book, but you realize you've never really connected with him or begun following him in the life-changing way you could. Guidance on this is available on request.
3. **You can be baptized.** Jesus was baptized to mark the inauguration of his revolution. Your baptism can make public your commitment to be part of what Jesus began, and to identify with his death and resurrection. Information on how and where to be baptized is available on request.
4. **You can join with others.** Jesus may have called individuals to follow him, but he sent them out two by two and always envisioned them being part of a community. Being a follower of Jesus is never a simple matter of having a private religion. Information on churches or groups you might consider joining is available on request.
5. **You can read the rest of the Bible.** This book was never intended to replace the Bible, but to whet your appetite for it. The story of Jesus is at the center of God's revelation: everything that came before leads up to it; everything that came afterward flows out of it. Reading plans and study guides are available on request.

6. **You can give this book to someone.** Individual copies are available on Amazon. Email the author for information on purchasing multiple copies at a discount.
7. **You can discuss this book.** The reflection questions included in each section can lead to great discussions with another person or in a small group. This may be the easiest and most natural form of evangelism and discipleship you've ever encountered. Information on starting or joining a group is available on request.
8. **You can do nothing.** Maybe someone gave you this book and told you to read it. You've done what you were asked to do, but nothing more. Maybe you're done. Or maybe not.
9. **You can read this book again.** Many have read the story of Jesus over and over, finding something new in it every time. This is what it means to say Scripture is inspired: God breathed into it as it was written and God breathes out of it as it is read.

The choice is yours, but if you'd like help with any of these steps, or for other questions or comments you may have, feel free to contact the author via email or on Facebook:

EncounteringJesusToday@gmail.com

Facebook Page: Encountering Jesus Today

Acknowledgments

Although this book reflects my interest in evangelism and discipleship over the past fifty years, the idea for it grew more recently out of my ministry as pastor of the First Baptist Church of Kalamazoo, Michigan. I have been privileged in this church to be involved with a number of creative mission intern projects, several of which brought me into contact with people who knew little about Jesus.

My career in pastoral ministry has always emphasized Scripture, but it has also been plagued by unease at how little grasp church members have of the Bible. (Perhaps this is the reason it has been called "the world's least read best seller.") Most people have a few favorite verses and a general familiarity with various stories, but get a "deer in the headlights" look when asked to describe the overall story of the Bible or even the story of Jesus told in the gospels.

Encountering Jesus Today: Revolution and Resurrection is intended for those who may never have read an entire gospel, much less all four gospels, or for those who have read them, but had trouble connecting with them. The content of this book is the story of Jesus as told by the gospel writers: Matthew, Mark, Luke and John. Nothing has been added to what they wrote, and nothing has been taken away, though much has been simplified and paraphrased to aid the reader. The text is based on the World English Bible (WEB), a revised and updated edition of the American Standard Version first published in 1901. Because the WEB is in the public domain, it could be used and paraphrased here without creating copyright issues.

Encountering Jesus Today: Revolution and Resurrection is not a harmony of the gospels determined to resolve all differences and discrepancies between the various accounts of the same events. My own sense is that these are not "errors" within the gospels, but the kind of richness expected from independent witnesses writing for different audiences and with different purposes in mind.

I owe a debt of gratitude to many people for their help with this project. I especially want to thank the following:

- The members of the First Baptist Church of Kalamazoo who have entrusted me with the leadership of their church at a critical time;
- The Wednesday morning Bible study group whose members have contributed to many lively discussions on the story of Jesus: Lisa Andrews, Jim Cooper, Sally Crouch, Catherine Dance, Kay Fisk, Candy Gejji, Nina Hamlin, Lori Lewis, Norm Lyons, Cal Mastin, Melanie Roenigk, and Susan Van Dis;
- Sara Kozminske a mission intern at our church, and her wonderful daughters, Hannah Flatt, Mary Kurzava and Sheila Kurzava, for their willingness to contribute artwork to the project;
- Marcy Mein, our church administrator, for bringing her expertise as a retired English teacher to bear on what I've written;
- Emily Worline, a mission intern at our church, student at Kalamazoo College and founder of Refugee Outreach Kalamazoo (ROK), and Syd Fernandez, her missionary partner at ROK for conversations in my office leading to this book;
- Lisa Andrews, a mission intern at our church, for the frankness she has always brought to our discussions from the perspective of someone who did not grow up in a church context;
- Our church's other mission interns for 2016, Chioma Atueyi, Catherine Dance, Karuna Khanal, and Chris Wahmhoff for keeping me engaged and energized by their creative ideas;
- Melanie Roenigk for excellent insights as a proofreader and her willingness to check all the scripture references for accuracy;
- Amanda Macarrao, my daughter (and a missionary in Mozambique), for designing the cover; and,
- Linnea Berg, my wife and number one editor, for her encouragement and insights at every step of the project.